THE FIVE-STRING BANJO PRIMER

If A Is May, F# Must Be February

by Joe Taschetta

IOWA STATE UNIVERSITY PRESS, *Ames,* IOWA

ABOUT THE AUTHOR

Joe Taschetta holds a B.S. degree in electrical engineering from Iowa State University and has held positions as a design engineer and as a college professor in that field. Upon returning to Iowa State and receiving a M.S. degree in education in 1978, he has turned to doing ''what I have always wanted''—pursuing the musical career that has intrigued him from the ''folk boom'' time of the early 1960s when he taught himself to play banjo and guitar. Taschetta has given instruction in these instruments to all ages with emphasis on folk music and its history. He has led a series of residencies for the ''artist-in-the-schools'' program sponsored by the Iowa Arts Council and has appeared widely as a touring folk musician in the Midwest.

Illustrations prepared by the author.

© 1979, 1978 by Joe Taschetta
All rights reserved

Composed and printed by The Iowa State University Press, Ames, Iowa 50010

Second edition, 1979

International Standard Book Number: 0-8138-0905-3

CONTENTS

PREFACE

WITH the trends toward the popular bluegrass five-string banjo songs "Bonnie and Clyde" and "Deliverance," many banjo pickers have learned by imitation alone. They have become extremely talented "technicians." If these pickers had learned the fundamental theories of music, especially with today's enthusiasm for this instrument, there could be a more rapid evolution of five-string banjo music. I hope my book will help fill this void.

The method of this book is the application of "praxeology" or the "study of doing." Practice without praxeology will usually have adverse effects, since it is not based on theory. The "whys" as well as the "hows" must be learned to truly understand any subject. It is my belief that once students understand music theory they can apply it to endless mechanical possibilities evolving from their interpretations and ingenuity. Thus through the format of this book the student will be introduced to the most basic laws of music and can immediately apply them in a practical way to an exercise or song lesson.

I will build these theories and laws from a concept old in thought but revolutionary in its application to fretted string instruments—that of the "Chromatic Circle Cycle."

This book has been written with the adult in mind. Many grew up as I did, fearing music. Only a chosen few seemed to be "musically talented" in school, and the rest were discouraged because of lack of this talent. In short, this book is for the guy who found out too late, because of our educational system, how much beauty and fun can be found in the world of music.

If you have the concept that music is too difficult to learn because you have waited too long, this book is written for you. If you don't know a C note from a G note, then all the better because the book starts at the base of understanding, the alphabet, and builds from there on observations gained from various levels of newly discovered theories.

A book on theory alone can get mighty boring; but this one uses "the study of doing" to apply derived musical theories and the development of psychomotor skills to one of the most unique instruments in America, the five-string banjo.

Anatomy of a Five-String Banjo

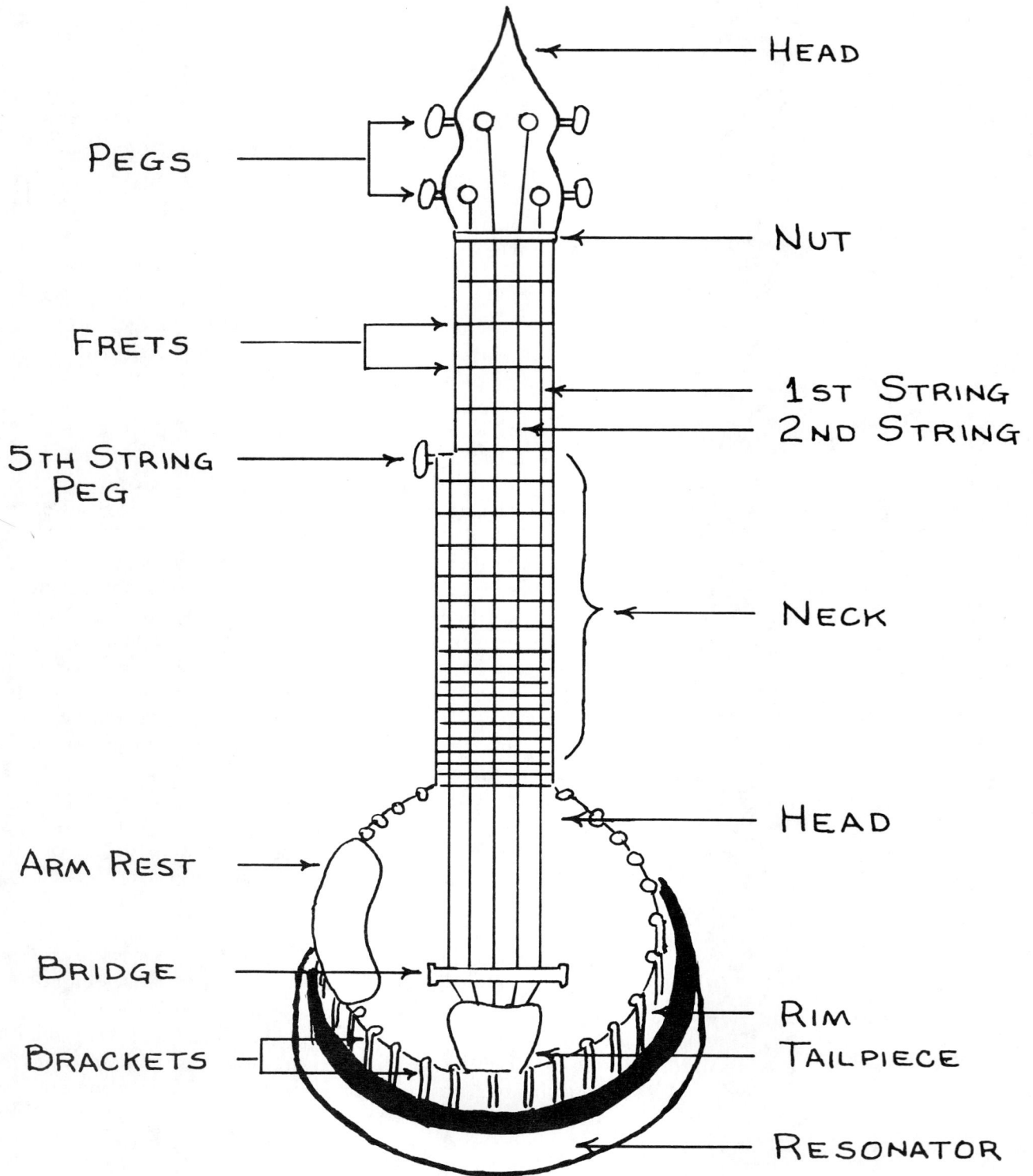

PEGS

FRETS

5TH STRING
PEG

ARM REST

BRIDGE

BRACKETS

HEAD

NUT

1ST STRING
2ND STRING

NECK

HEAD

RIM
TAILPIECE

RESONATOR

The Half-step Theory

There are 12 "half steps" (or notes) in our music system, lettered from A to G. Here is how the system works. The 12 half steps are as follows:

```
1  2   3  4   5  6   7  8 9  10  11 12  1
A  A#  B  C   C# D   D# E  F  F#  G  G#  A . . .
```

(Note: "#" is read "sharp"; that is, A# = A sharp.) When you come to A again (the note after 12), you repeat the same sequence but now you are an octave higher. The word "octave" has the Latin root *"oct"* meaning eight. To go up an octave means to go up eight tones; that is,

```
 1   2   3   4    5    6   7   8
do   re  mi  fa  sol  la  ti  do
```

Remember how you sang the scales in music class? This eight-tone scale will be amplified later in this book when we discuss the major diatonic scale.

Frequency as Applied to Musical Notes

In scientific lingo when you go up an octave, the "frequency" is exactly doubled. Going up an octave also means going up 12 half steps. Let's see what happens when we go from an A note to another A note that is an octave higher than the first.

An A note, as defined by the National Bureau of Standards in Washington, D.C., has a frequency of 220 cycles per second. We already know what a "second" is (basic unit of time) and what a "per" is (for each), but what is a "cycle"? Look at Figure 1, which shows one cycle of an A note.

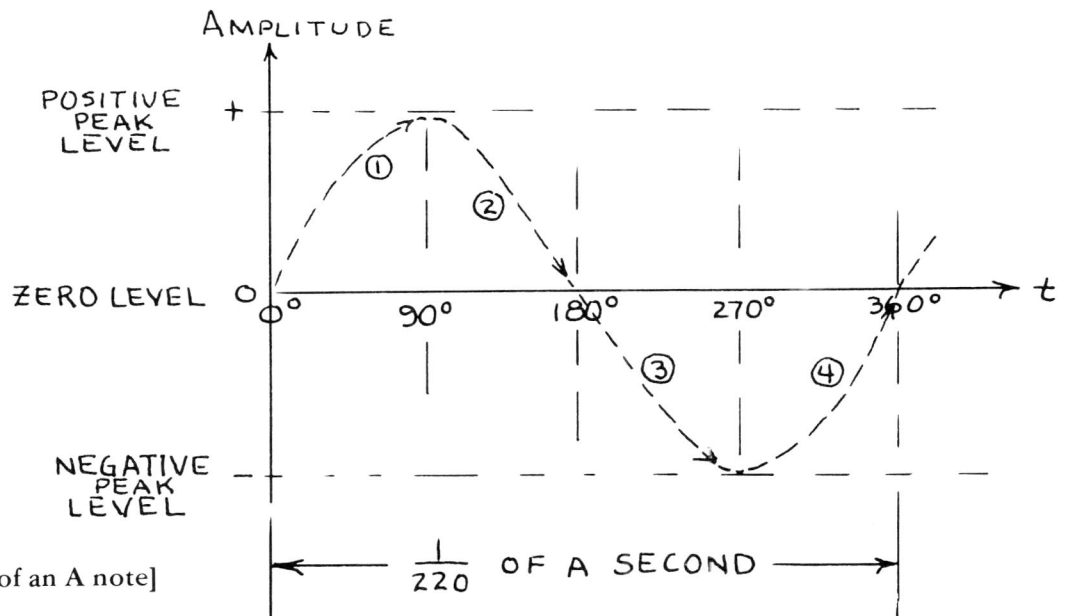

[Fig. 1. One cycle of an A note]

One complete cycle has the following four parts:

- From 0° to 90°—the amplitude starts at the zero level and goes up to the positive peak level.
- From 90° to 180°—the amplitude goes from the positive peak back to zero.
- From 180° to 270°—the amplitude goes from the zero level to the negative peak level.
- From 270° to 360°—the amplitude goes from the negative peak level back to the zero level.

The second cycle would repeat the same pattern, and so on for the next cycle. This pattern is a trigonometric function called the sinusoidal wave. Now, since the note A has 220 cycles per second for its frequency, it will be reproduced when 220 of these "cycles" occur in one second.

To go an octave higher from this A note, the frequency would be doubled (220 cycles per second × 2 = 440 cycles per second). This 440 cycle per second tone is an A note that is now an octave higher than the previous one.

The Chromatic Circle Cycle

The sequence of 12 half steps (HS) is repeated for every octave. Since this is a repetition, we can liken the half steps to the system of keeping time on our clocks. In both cases we have what is known as a "modulus of twelve": let A represent 12 o'clock, A# represent 1 o'clock, B

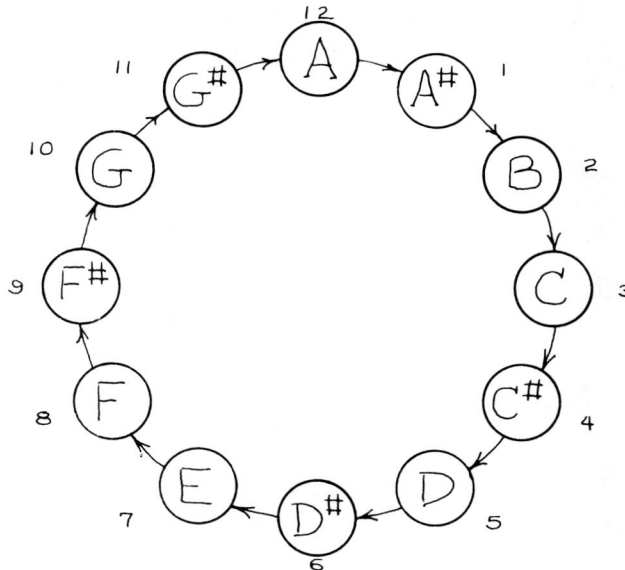

[Fig. 2]

2

represent 2 o'clock, and so forth. For every octave we go up, we go around a full 12 hours, or one complete circle. I call this the "Chromatic Circle Cycle" (CCC). It is shown in Figure 2.

Although we have a wide range of notes to which ears are responsive (the audio frequency spectrum), there are still *only* 12 HS notes to be concerned about. We just go up or down in octaves, repeating the same 12 HS notes.

There is an easy way to remember all 12 half steps. First, memorize the alphabet from A to G. Second, remember there are no notes between B and C and E and F. All the other notes (letters) have in-between notes; for instance, between A and B there is A#, B and C there is nothing, C and D there is C#, D and E there is D#, E and F there is nothing, F and G there is F#, and G and A there is G#, and start all over again.

Note that we have been going "up" (increasing frequency) on the scale. That is the reason for all the sharps. "Sharp" means "above" your reference. For instance, A# is a higher note (higher frequency) than A.

Now what happens if we go "down" (decrease frequency) on the scale? In music, to go down you go "flat" (shown as ♭). All the in-between notes that were sharp going up are now flat going down. Going up the scale, we went clockwise around the circle. Going down the scale, we will be going counterclockwise.

So how will the CCC look going down? Almost the same as going up except the names of the sharps will be changed to protect the innocent. In other words, E and F and B and C still have no in-between notes and the others are now called flats.

Look at Figure 3. We now go backward through the alphabet from G to A. What was an A# (above A) in Figure 2 has now been transformed into a B♭ (below B), and so on around the circle. The completed CCC with all the corresponding sharps and flats is shown in Figure 4.

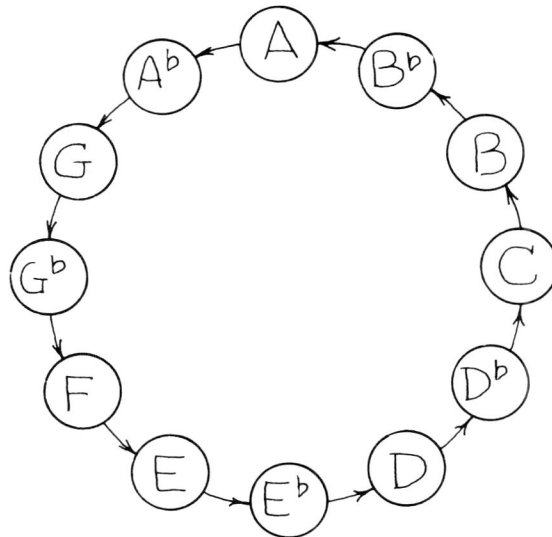

[Fig. 3]

3

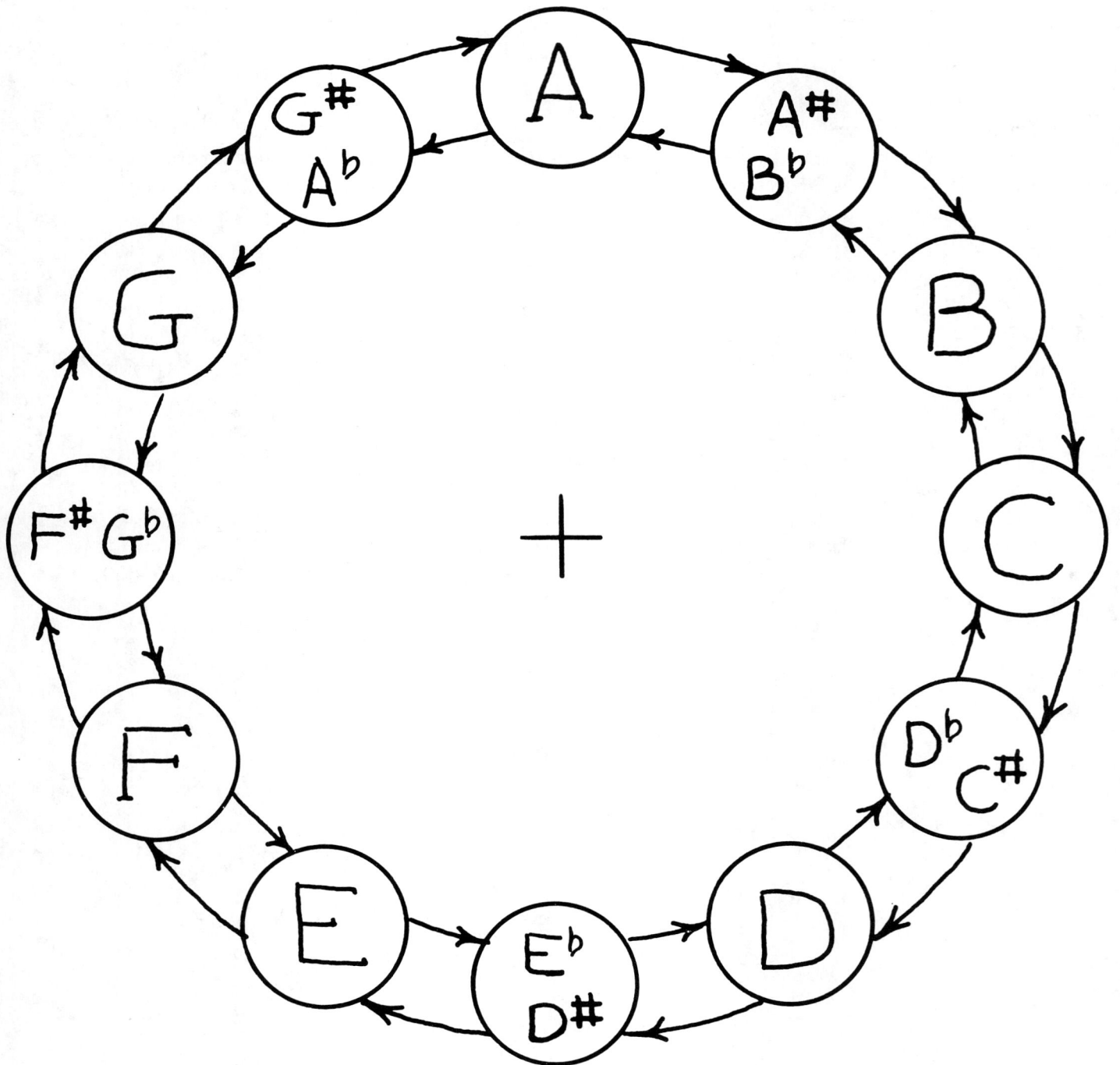

[Fig. 4. The twelve half steps of the CCC]

Tuning Up

You may be asking yourself, "But what does all this half-step stuff mean?" That's a very good question. To a stringed instrument with frets, like the banjo, it means everything:

- Going up a *half step* is *equal* to
- Moving up *one fret* on the banjo

So the banjo now becomes a half-step instrument. I like that. All the notes look the same on a banjo. It's a liberated instrument, unlike the piano which still discriminates between its "white" notes and those other "black" notes!

OPEN-G TUNING

Now let's look at the banjo fingerboard in Figure 5 and practice some tuning techniques.

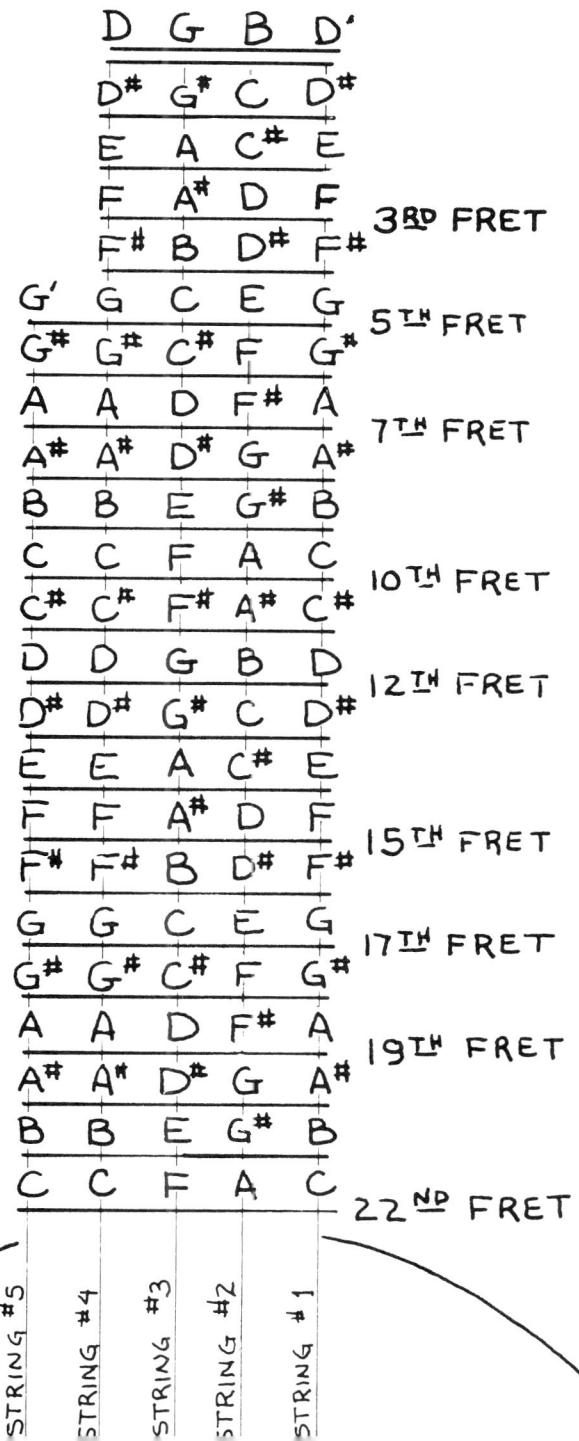

	D	G	B	D'	
	D#	G#	C	D#	
	E	A	C#	E	
	F	A#	D	F	
	F#	B	D#	F#	3RD FRET
G'	G	C	E	G	5TH FRET
G#	G#	C#	F	G#	
A	A	D	F#	A	7TH FRET
A#	A#	D#	G	A#	
B	B	E	G#	B	
C	C	F	A	C	
C#	C#	F#	A#	C#	10TH FRET
D	D	G	B	D	
D#	D#	G#	C	D#	12TH FRET
E	E	A	C#	E	
F	F	A#	D	F	
F#	F#	B	D#	F#	15TH FRET
G	G	C	E	G	
G#	G#	C#	F	G#	17TH FRET
A	A	D	F#	A	
A#	A#	D#	G	A#	19TH FRET
B	B	E	G#	B	
C	C	F	A	C	22ND FRET

[Fig. 5. Banjo fingerboard—open-G tuning]

STRING #5 STRING #4 STRING #3 STRING #2 STRING #1

To tune the banjo, start by tuning the fourth string to the D below the piano's middle C. This note can be found from another tuned banjo, a piano, a tuning fork, or a pitch pipe. The string is tuned by plucking it with your right-hand thumb. The thumb plucks the string in a downward motion about *3 inches from the bridge.* Don't be timid; pluck the string hard enough to make it resonate (vibrate). While the string is resonating, tune it to the proper pitch. Adjust tension by turning the peg. *Remember:* Tighter tension gives higher notes; looser tension gives lower notes.

When tuning, pluck the string first, then tune it. Many times a beginner will tune the string first, then pluck it to see if it is there yet. It is far easier to hear where you're going than where you've been! For most folks, it is easier to tune ''up'' to a desired note than ''down'' to it. Start with the string to be tuned below the pitch desired, then tune it up to the note.

After the fourth (or D) string is tuned, go to the fifth fret (five half steps) on that string. See Figure 6 for the proper location of the left-hand social finger for fretting ''up the neck'' (frets are counted ''up'' toward the bridge). As shown, place the finger just before the fret; for example, to play the fourth string at the fifth fret, place the finger between frets 4 and 5, about one-third the distance from the fifth fret. You will be playing the G note, which is what the third string open should be tuned to. (''Open'' means played open, that is, no fingers on the frets.)

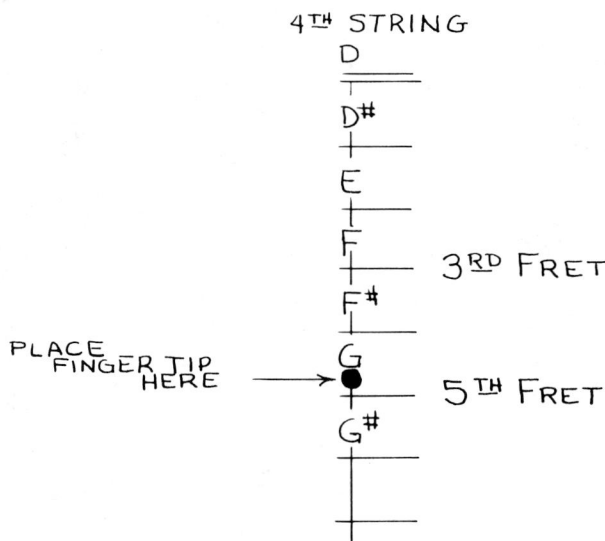

[Fig. 6]

Tune the third string to this G note. After the third (G) string is tuned, go to the fourth fret (four half steps) on that string and pluck the note B, which is what the second string open is to be tuned to. After the second string is tuned to B, go to the third fret on the string and play the D note. Now tune the first string open to this note. The first-string D note is an octave higher than the fourth-string D note. The higher D is shown as D′ in Figure 5 (this is called ''D prime'').

Finally, go to the fifth fret on the first string and sound the G note. Now tune the fifth string open to that note. The fifth string is an octave higher than the third-string G. It is shown as G′ in Figure 5.

If you have done all this right, your banjo should now be tuned as shown in Figure 7. The banjo is now tuned to what is called an "open-G tuning"; that is, if you strum across all five strings open, a G major chord will sound. More on chords later.

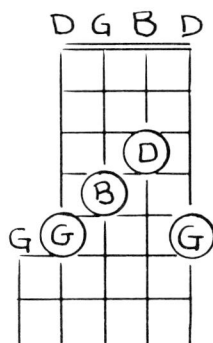

[Fig. 7]

It is often difficult for the untrained ear to determine if the string being tuned is sharp or flat from the desired note. By "relative tuning" you can determine this. For example, the third string open should be tuned to a G note. Let's say you are not sure if the string is sharp or flat from the G note sounded from the fourth string at the fifth fret. If the third string open matches a note above the fifth fret on the fourth string, you're sharp, so tune the third string down (lower the pitch; that is, loosen the string with the peg). If the third string open matches a note below the fifth fret of the fourth string, you're flat. Tune the third string up (raise the pitch; that is, tighten the string with the peg).

EXERCISE—*Tuning Practice*

Keep the fourth string (D) in tune and lower strings 1, 2, 3, and 5. Practice tuning these strings over and over until you get a feel for the relative notes. Be *patient. Listen* to what you're doing. You must now develop a sense of pitch. This comes with much practice and concentration. If you have to, lock yourself in the bedroom closet so no one bothers you or vice-versa.

For another exercise, fill in all the notes for the blank fingerboard in Figure 8. Again, think half steps. (Figure 5 has the answers.)

Before going any further in this book, be sure you can tune the banjo with relative ease. It is important to know *why* you're tuning the banjo as well as *how* to tune it. Above all else, *be patient.* Each person learns at his or her own rate, so don't go comparing yourself with other banjo pickers. Playing a musical instrument is for enjoyment, not for competition.

A final note on tuning: if the banjo doesn't sound right once it is tuned, check the position of the bridge. The distance from the nut to the twelfth fret should be the same distance as from that fret to the bridge.

7

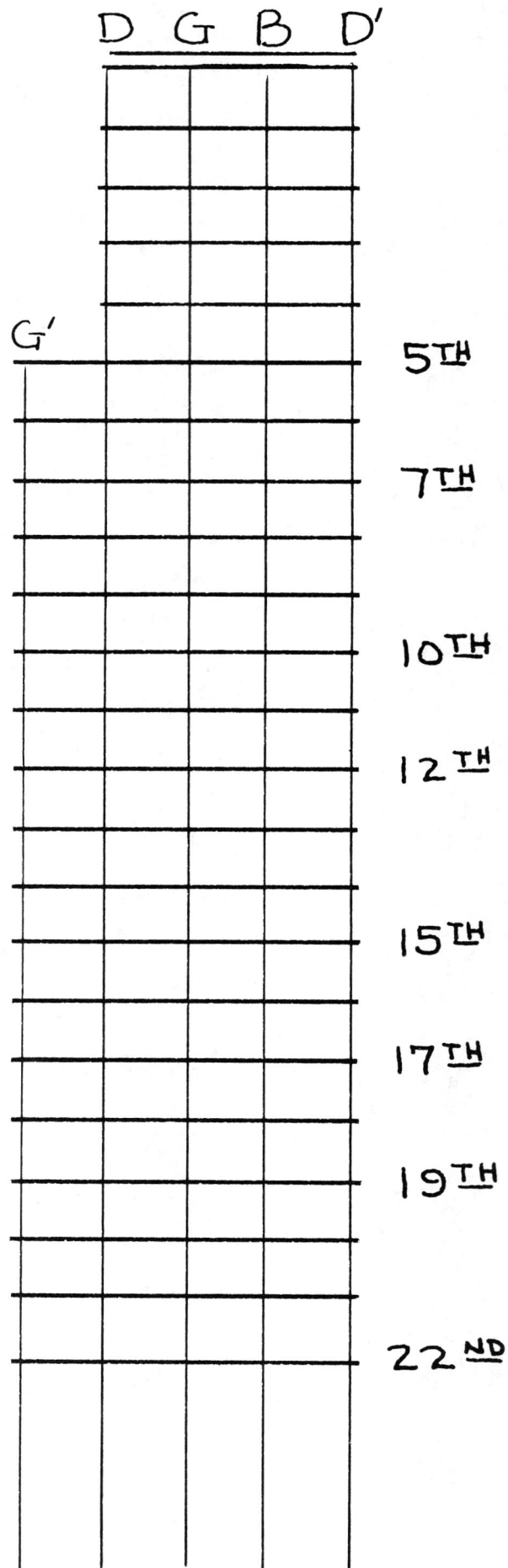

[Fig. 8]

The Left Hand

The left hand is used in fingering the frets of the banjo. Figure 9 gives the name (and number) of each finger.

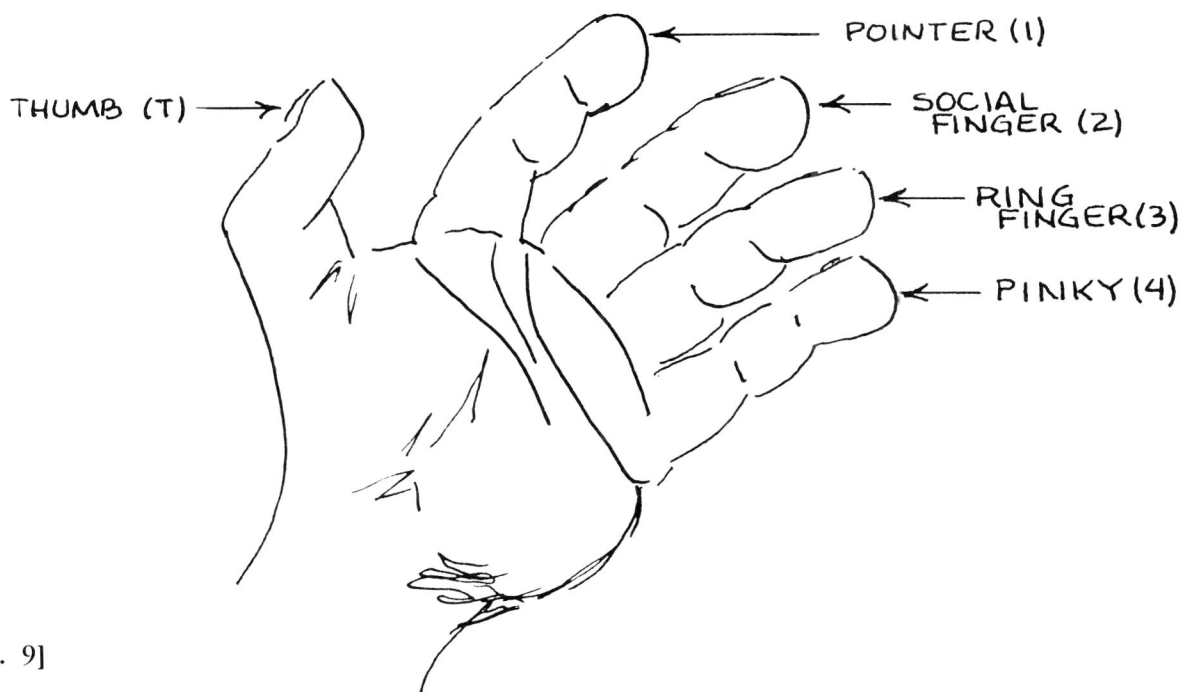

THUMB (T) →

POINTER (1)

SOCIAL FINGER (2)

RING FINGER (3)

PINKY (4)

[Fig. 9]

(Note: This book is written for the right-hander; all southpaws can simply substitute "right" for "left" hand and vice-versa. Many banjo manufacturers produce left-handed banjos, which are the mirror image of right-handed ones. However, this is not an absolute necessity for southpaws since many can easily learn to play the standard instrument, that is, learn to play right-handed.)

Left-hand fingernails *must be cut way down!* The fingertips, *not* your fingernail, are to fret the string. After many hours of practicing and pain, the fingertips develop nice hard calluses, as in Figure 10. Don't expect to develop these overnight. They will evolve naturally after much *regular* practice.

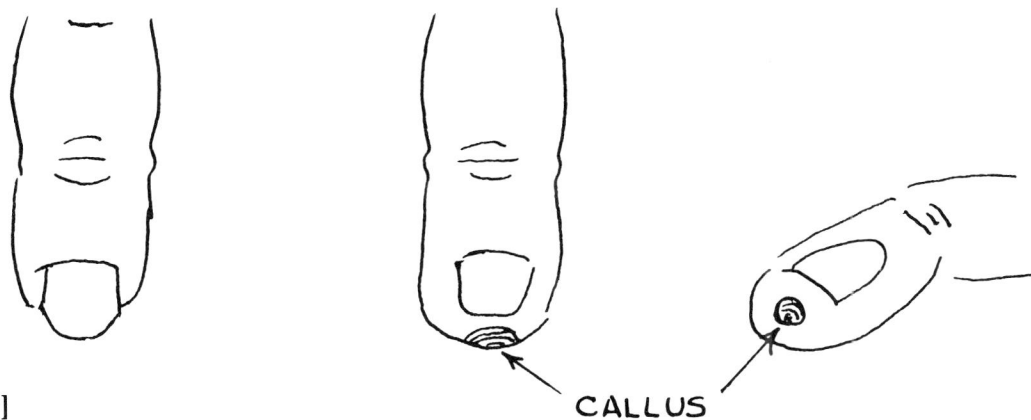

[Fig. 10]

CALLUS

9

The proper grasp on the neck of the banjo is extremely important if you are to have a clear, crisp sound. Make a "claw" with your left hand (Fig. 11) as if trying to hold a ball with your wrist. The fingers should (almost) be perpendicular to the fingerboard, over the appropriate strings between frets, to permit quick movement as you change finger positions.

When fretting the strings, use:

- Finger 1 (pointer) for fret 1
- Finger 2 (social) for fret 2
- Finger 3 (ring) for fret 3
- Finger 4 (pinky) for fret 4

[Fig. 11]

Fingers should press on the fingerboard toward the thumb, and the thumb should press up on the neck toward the fingers. Think of your left hand as a C-clamp. *Remember:* short fingernails!

CHORDS OF G, C, AND D7

Now with what you have learned try playing the basic chords of G, C, and D7. Before attempting this, review the methods for fretting (tuning) given earlier.

For the chords in the key of G major, the left-hand fingers should be placed as given below (see Fig. 9 for finger numbers):

Chord	String number	Finger number	Fret number
G major chord (G)	All 5 strings are played *open* for the G chord		
C major chord (C)	1	3	2
	2	1	1
	4	2	2
D7 chord (D7)	2	1	1
	3	2	2

Figure 12 shows the above chords in standard diagram form.

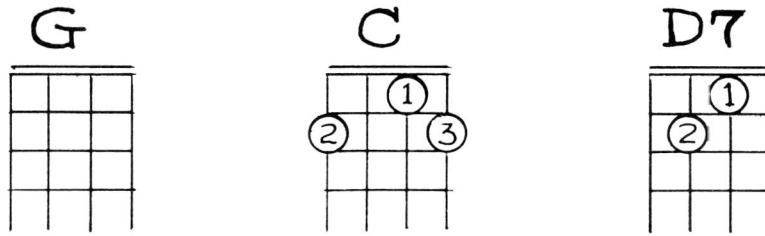

[Fig. 12]

After selecting the desired chord with the fingers of your left hand. pluck each string separately with your right thumb. If each string doesn't sound crisp and clear, look at your left-hand fingers that are doing the fretting and correct whatever finger (or fingers) may be causing the undesired sound.

After each string sounds clear, strum down on all the strings in one quick motion with your thumb. You have played a *chord,* which is simply *a special combination of several notes.* More on the "whys" of chords later.

The Right Hand

The right hand is used for playing the strings of the banjo. The numbers and names assigned to fingers are the same as those for the left hand (Fig. 9). The right hand can be used for two distinct styles. The first is "strumming" across the strings; the second is "picking" individual strings.

FINGER PICKS

You may want to try using finger picks, which will allow you to get more sound from your banjo. Use a plastic thumb pick and metal finger picks for best results. The thumb pick should fit snugly and not protrude more than ¼ to ⅜ inch from the end of your thumb.

I personally prefer the feel of "Ernie Ball" finger picks, but others are also satisfactory. Contour the pick so it goes toward your fingernail.

To prevent your finger pick from flying all over the place as you are picking away, hold it down with a thin strip of electrician's tape (the cloth kind, not plastic) around the base of the pick above the first knuckle. (See Fig. 13.) Bend the pick slightly off center from your finger for better contact with the string, as shown in Figure 14.

[Fig. 13]

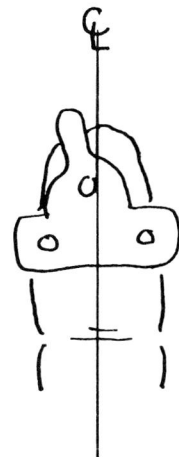

[Fig. 14]

11

Basic Strum

For the basic strum, draw your right thumb down across all strings, using a constant, slow melodic beat. While doing this, change chords with your left fingers as smoothly as possible. By all means, keep your right hand moving with this constant beat even if your left hand can't keep the pace at first. Your left hand will learn if you *practice, practice, practice! A constant beat is imperative!* Strum and change chords until you can do it smoothly, since it is extremely important to coordinate the two hands.

Don't be concerned if you can't play a given lesson as fast and smoothly as you would like. Speed comes only with much practice. The speed alone does not make a good player, it is the quality that counts. Concentrate on clarity and steady rhythm, the rest evolves with practice.

Remember it is better to practice 15 minutes a day for a week than to practice 2 hours all in one day.

Now try strumming a few songs. The following pages have four old standards that almost everyone knows. In the first two the chords to be played are circled. For example, in "On Top of Old Smoky" the G chord is played for the words "On top of Old," then the C chord is played for the words "Smoky, all covered with," then back to the G chord for "snow, I lost my true," and so on, following the marked chords to the end.

For each arrow pointing down, strum down on all five strings with your right thumb. Keep each down strum at the same constant beat. In our example, "On," "top," "of," and "old" each get one strum down, whereas "Smo-" gets three strums down and "ky" gets five strums down.

The songs "Worried Man Blues" and "Can the Circle Be Unbroken" show the chord notation you are more likely to see in a regular music book. No arrows are given, so the strumming is left to the student's interpretation.

EXERCISE—*Strumming Practice*

On Top of Old Smoky

12

My Bonnie Lies over the Ocean

(G) My Bon- nie lies o- ver the (C) o- (G) cean
My Bon- nie lies o- ver the (D7) sea
My (G) Bon- nie lies o- ver the (C) o- (G) cean
Please bring back my (D7) Bon- nie to me (G)
(G) Bring back, (C) bring back, Oh, (D7) bring back
My Bon- nie (G) to me to me
Bring back, (C) bring back, Oh, (D7) bring back
My Bon- (G) nie to me

Worried Man Blues

G
It takes a worried man to sing a worried song
  C   **G**
It takes a worried man to sing a worried song

It takes a worried man to sing a worried song
                D7   **G**
I'm worried now, but I won't be worried long.

I went down the valley, and I lay me down to sleep (3 times)
When I awoke, I had shackles on my feet.

I asked the judge, what's gonna be my fine (3 times)
Twenty-one years, on the Hard Rock Mountain line.

Twenty-one years I paid for that awful crime (3 times)
Then I found out, he gave me ninety-nine.

If anyone should ask you, who did write this song (3 times)
Say it 'twas I, and I sing it all day long.

Can the Circle Be Unbroken?

G
I was standing by the window
        C   **G**
On one cold and cloudy day:

And I saw the hearse come rolling
              D7   **G**
For to carry my mother away

Chorus:
G
Can the circle be unbroken?
      C   **G**
Bye and bye, Lord, bye and bye.

There's a better home a-waiting
            D7 **G**
In the sky, Lord, in the sky.

Lord, I told the undertaker,
"Undertaker, please drive slow:
For this body you are hauling,
Lord, I hate to see her go."

Lord, I followed close behind her,
Tried to stand up and be brave:
But I could not hide my sorrow
When they laid her in the grave.

Went back home, Lord, my home was lonesome
Since my mother she was gone:
All my brothers, sisters crying,
What a home so sad and lone.

.

    Strumming down with just your thumb can get boring mighty quickly. For a change try strumming down with your thumb first, then make a very light brush up (strum), with finger 1 over the higher strings (that is, strings 1, 2, and 3). When brushing up with the finger, remember that not all five strings have to be strummed. Finger 1 (pointer) uses the same action to brush the strings as that to scratch your head.

    Try playing the same songs again but this time strum "down-up" rather than just "down." *With practice,* you will soon have a special strum technique for each new song you learn.

Go to your local music store and find some songs that you enjoy. Make your practicing fun by learning the songs that *you* like. Be sure the music you buy has the simple melody line and chord accompaniment for the songs. Learning to read music will be discussed later.

One of the best and cheapest sources of folk songs I have come across is *Reprints from Sing Out Magazine*. Each reprint (there are 11) has about 60 songs and costs only $1.50 per volume. The address is Sing Out!, 505 8th Ave., New York, NY 10018.

Other good source books for songs include: *American Favorite Ballads* by Pete Seeger, *Folksinger's Wordbook* by Fred and Irwin Silber, and *Folk Songs of North America* by John and Alan Lomax.

If you don't have the money or can't find any of the above books, try your local library. I am always amazed at the fine selections of music that libraries have. Some of the books are priceless.

Above everything else, pick a book with songs you like and want to learn. It doesn't matter if the music is folk, bluegrass, blues, gospel, or hard-core rock; the five-string banjo lends itself to all forms. Just make sure the chords, melody lines (treble clef), and (hopefully) words are given for each song.

This variety can aid in coordinating the three prime ingredients for playing a song on the banjo—your right hand, your left hand, and your voice.

The Treble Clef

Real honest-to-goodness notes are played on the banjo. If you want to learn the instrument properly and with any kind of depth, you must learn to read music. You can still play by ear and you don't have to read well, but it sure does help.

The notes on the banjo can be read from the "treble clef" scale. The treble clef has five lines called a "staff." The treble clef sign on the staff looks like a fancy script G. The treble clef is also called the "G clef" because the second line up is the G note. (See Fig. 15.) The notes played on the treble clef are the treble (higher) notes as opposed to the "bass clef," which contains bass notes that are below middle C. In other words, the bass clef is below the treble clef. Note that the lower part of the treble clef sign circles around the second line (G).

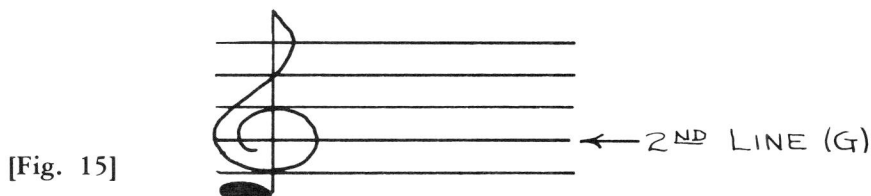

[Fig. 15]   ←— 2ND LINE (G)

The lines on the treble clef are lettered E, G, B, D, and F going up. This can be remembered by the phrase "Every Good Boy Does Fine." The spaces spell "FACE" going up (Fig. 16). *Learn to read the proper note belonging to each space and line.* This is the first step in reading music.

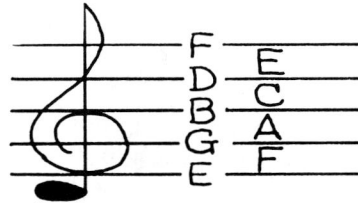

[Fig. 16]

There is nothing really mysterious about the order of notes. The bottom line starts at E, and for each adjacent space or line you go up one letter of the alphabet of the musical scale; that is, E, F, G, A, B, C, D, E, F. By this sequence, what is the space above the top line F? (G, of course.) Now, what is the space note below the bottom line E? (D, right?) This D is the note just above the "middle C."

LOCATION OF BANJO NOTES

Figure 17 pictures the notes of the treble clef as they are located on the banjo. Play these notes from D (fourth string open) to G (fifth string open). Do these notes agree with the fingerboard diagram in Figure 5? *Before going any further in this book, be sure you know where these "whole tones" are located with respect to each string and fret. Commit these notes to memory.* PRACTICE!

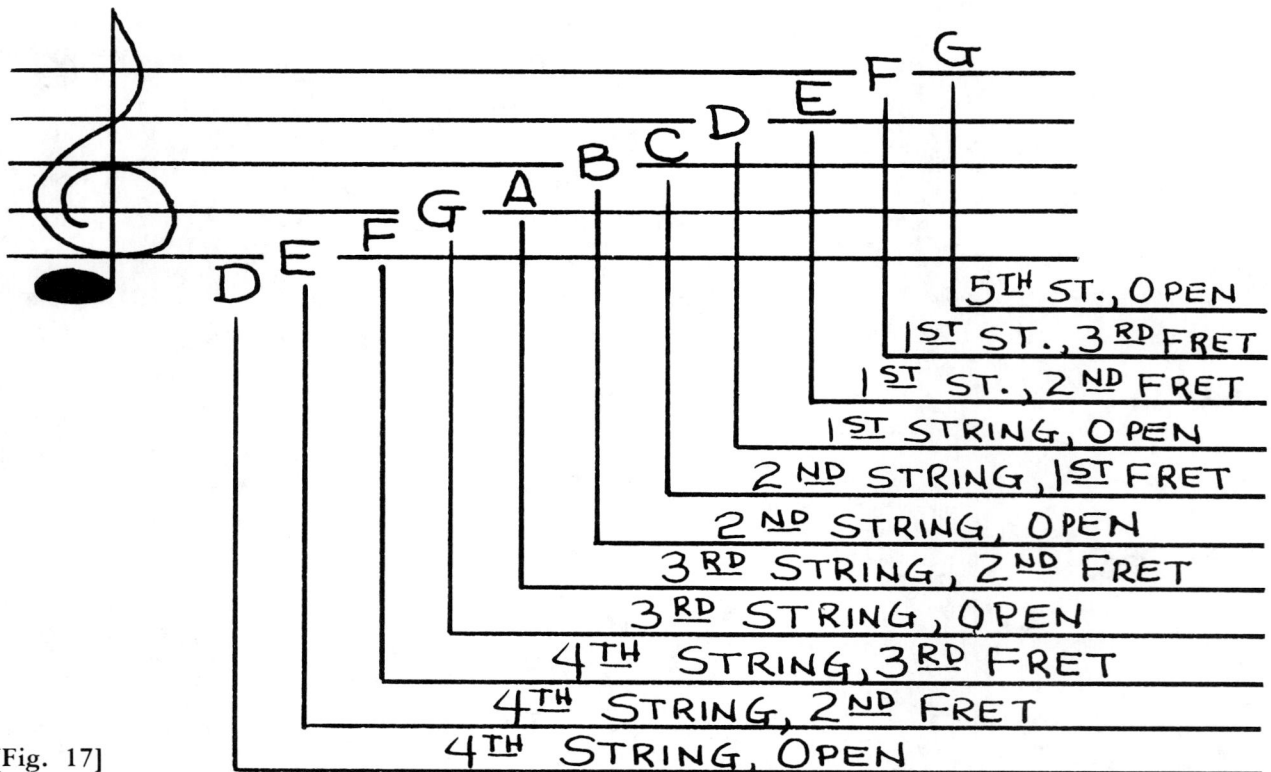

[Fig. 17]

16

EXERCISE—*Playing the Scale for the Key of G Major*

The most popular "key" played on the five-string banjo is the key of G major. The most obvious reason for this is that the banjo is tuned to open-G tuning.

In the key of G, the F note is played F#. *Remember:* F# is up one half step (one fret) from the whole tone F. All the other notes for the key of G are played by the remaining whole tones. In other words, the key of G has the following notes in it: G, A, B, C, D, E, F#, G.

A sharp sign is indicated on the top line (F) of the treble clef scale to indicate that F# rather than F is to be played for the key of G (Fig. 18). This now becomes the "key signature" for the key of G.

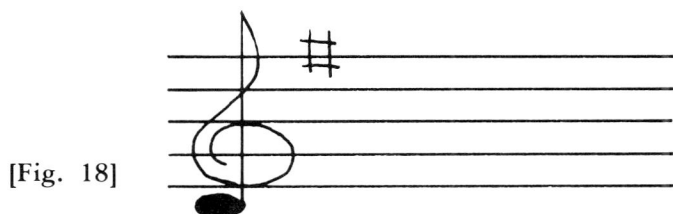

[Fig. 18]

As an exercise draw the treble clef for the key of G showing the following:

● Lines of the staff.
● Treble clef sign.
● Key signature for the key of G.
● Notes on the treble clef for the key of G from the fourth-string D note to the fifth-string G note.
● Location of each note with respect to the string and fret.

Answer to exercise:

NOTE	D	E	F#	G	A	B	C	D	E	F#	G
STRING	4	4	4	4/3	3	3/2	2	2/1	1	1	1/5
FRET	0	2	4	5/0	2	4/0	1	3/0	2	4	5/0

[Fig. 19]

You can see from this exercise that the G note of the second line of the treble clef can be played on the third string open or on the fourth string at the fifth fret. The B note is played either on the second string open or on the third string at the fourth fret. The D′ note is played on the first string open or on the second string at the third fret. Finally, the G′ note is played on the first string at the fifth fret or on the fifth string open.

Because this exercise is in the key of G, F# rather than F is being played on the fourth string at the fourth fret and on the first string at the fourth fret.

EXERCISE—*Playing the Scale of G Major*

Now apply what you have just learned and play the scale in Figure 20. Call out the notes as you read them. Learn to identify the location of each note in the treble clef.

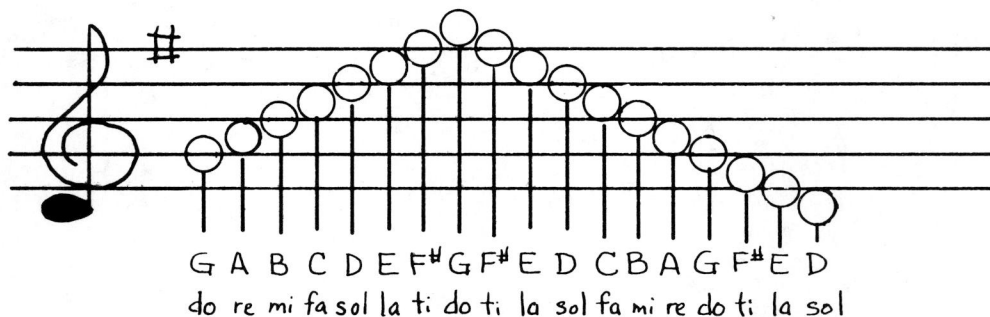

G A B C D E F# G F# E D C B A G F# E D

do re mi fa sol la ti do ti la sol fa mi re do ti la sol

[Fig. 20]

Many musicians just want to "play" the notes, they are not interested in reading them. Those old-timey musicians make a good point: music shouldn't be hampered by all those theories and note reading; it should just be *played*. However, to develop your skills and have a greater understanding of music, you must know some reading and theory to progress through your music lessons and practice sessions more efficiently. It is important to read music—at least well enough to decipher a new melody when you first see it.

When playing the scale in Figure 20, the first fret is fretted by the first finger (pointer) of the left hand; the second fret by the second finger (social); the third fret by the third finger (ring); and finally the fourth fret by the fourth finger (pinky). Pluck the string with your right thumb.

Before going any further in this book, practice the scale for the key of G forward and backward, looking and blindfolded. These are the "do, re, mi" notes that make up what is called "the major diatonic scale" for the key of G (discussed in detail later). What this simply means is that 99 percent of the songs in the key of G will have combinations of these eight notes in them. They are, as shown in Figure 20: do = G, re = A, mi = B, fa = C, sol = D, la = E, ti = F#, do = G.

Since most (at least many) of the songs you will be playing will be in the key of G, *practice until you know where the notes are.* This will help in "ad-libbing" or "jamming" the desired melody, since you will also know by omission what notes not to play for the key of G, that is, G#, A#, C#, D#, and F.

18

The Measure and Time Signature

A "measure" is the distance between two vertical lines, called "bar lines," on the staff. The "time signature" appears at the beginning measure of a song and has two parts, the numerator and the denominator, as 3/4 in Figure 21. If the timing changes during the song, another time signature will be given at that point.

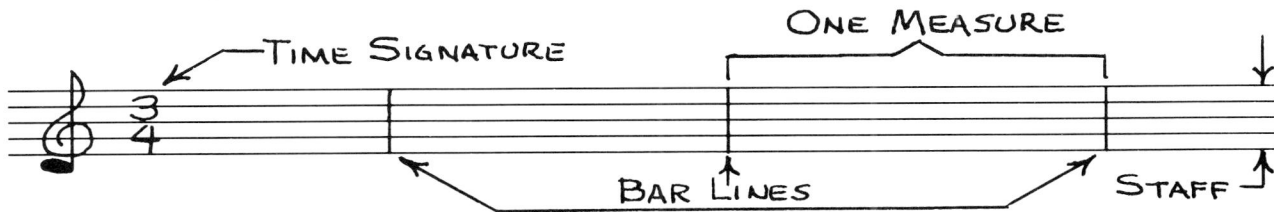

[Fig. 21]

The top number (numerator) of the time signature tells how many "whole beats" there are in each measure. The example tells us there are three (3) whole beats for one complete measure. *The bottom number (denominator) of the time signature indicates which note gets a whole beat.* In the example, a quarter note (1/4) would get one whole beat, an eighth note would get half a beat, a half note would get two whole beats, and a whole note would get four whole beats. This time signature is called "three-four" (3/4) time, as in a waltz.

NOTE TIMING PROPORTIONS

Notes are differentiated in the following ways:

- Eighth notes, quarter notes, half notes, and whole notes are shown in Figure 22A.
- Notes can be divided further by adding more flags (Fig. 22B).
- Stems on the notes point up for notes below the middle line of the treble clef (B) and down for notes B and above (Fig. 22C).
- Flags can be joined together for like notes (Fig. 22D).
- Dotted notes (length of note plus half) are shown in Figure 23.

Timing proportions of all these notes are given in Figure 23.

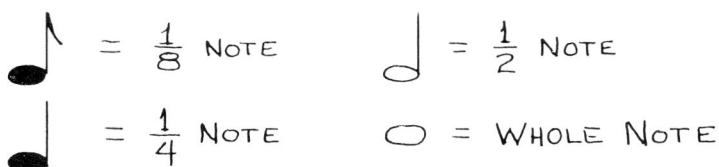

[Fig. 22A]

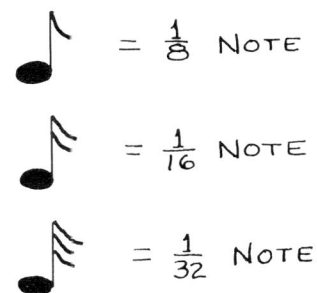

[Fig. 22B]

19

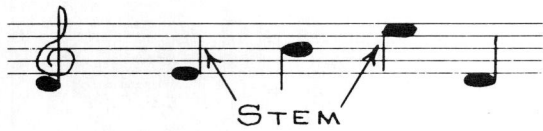

[Fig. 22C]

[Fig. 22D]

LET 1/8 NOTE = 1 SECOND

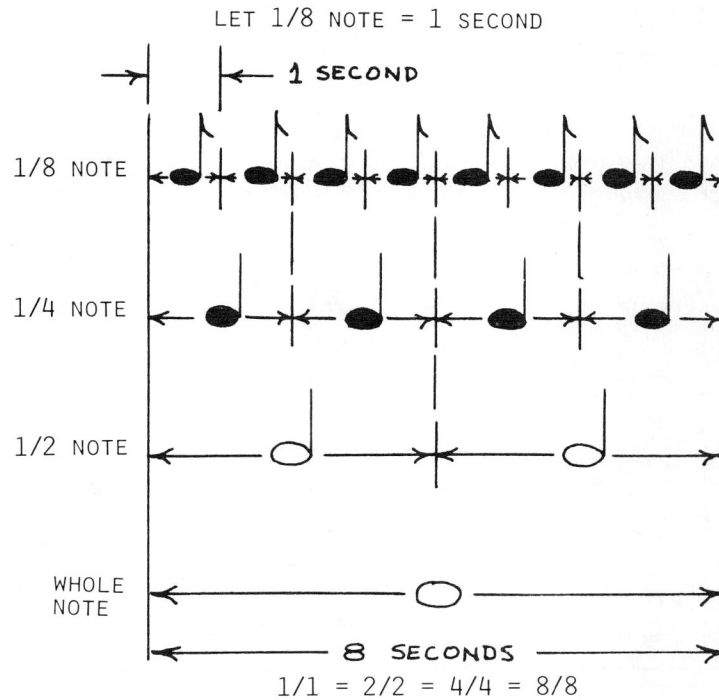

1/8 NOTE

1/4 NOTE

1/2 NOTE

WHOLE NOTE

8 SECONDS

1/1 = 2/2 = 4/4 = 8/8

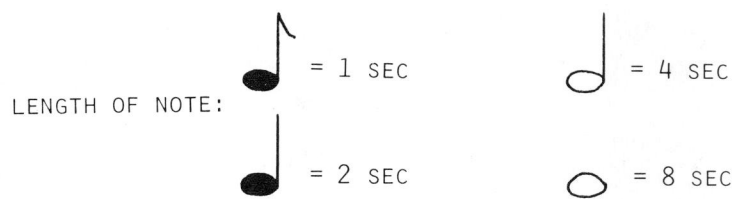

LENGTH OF NOTE:

= 1 SEC   = 4 SEC

= 2 SEC   = 8 SEC

DOTTED NOTE = LENGTH OF NOTE + HALF ITS LENGTH:

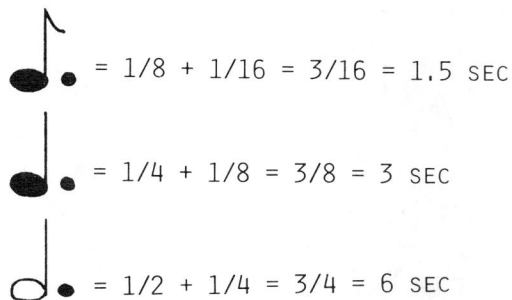

= 1/8 + 1/16 = 3/16 = 1.5 SEC

= 1/4 + 1/8 = 3/8 = 3 SEC

[Fig. 23. Note timing proportions]

= 1/2 + 1/4 = 3/4 = 6 SEC

20

EXERCISE—*Filling in Missing Note(s)*

Fill in the missing notes for each measure below:

Answer to exercise:

"TOM DOOLEY"

"Tom Dooley" is written in 4/4 time, which is "common" time (C). Each quarter note gets one whole beat, and there are four whole beats per measure (Fig. 24).

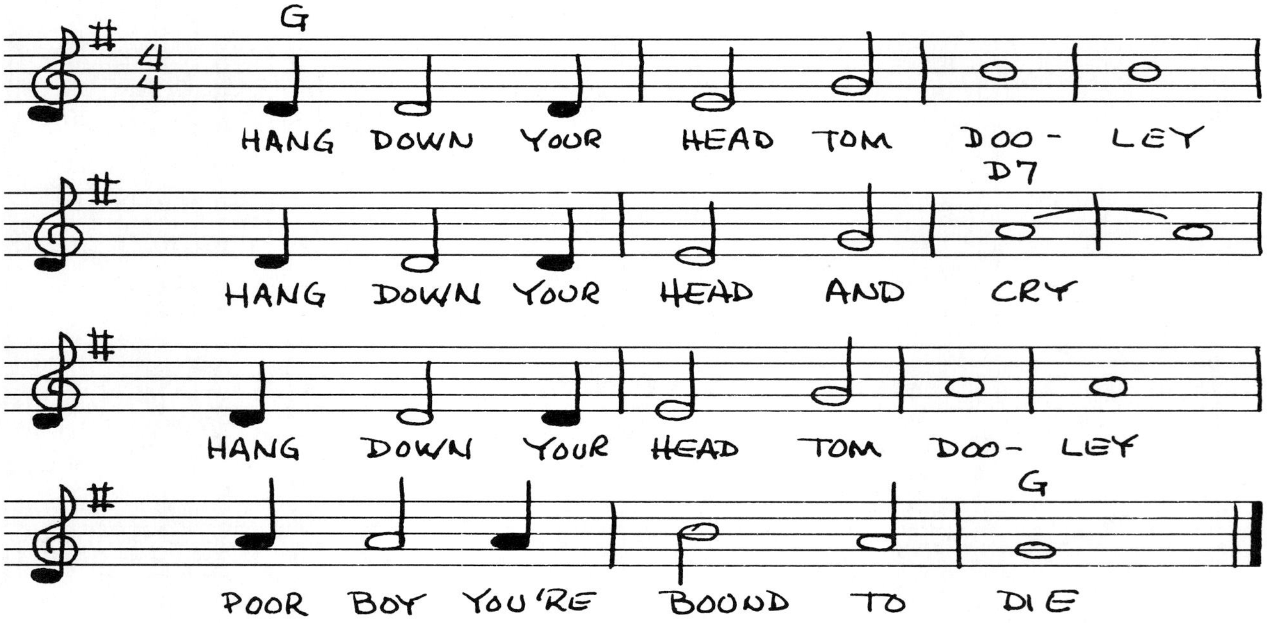

[Fig. 24]

EXERCISE—*Strumming "Tom Dooley"*

As an exercise strum through "Tom Dooley" using the chords of G and D7 as marked above the treble clef staff. (See Fig. 12 for chord diagrams.) The G chord is played from "Hang" to "and," then at "cry" the chord changes to D7, which is played for the remainder of the song until at "die" the last note is changed back to the G chord.

Each strum will be given a whole beat. Thus a quarter note gets one strum, a half note gets two strums, and a whole note gets four strums. How many strums for each measure? Why?

EXERCISE—*Playing the Melody for "Tom Dooley"*

Tap your foot and count four equal beats; this is one measure. A quarter note gets one beat, a half note gets two beats, and a whole note gets four beats. For example, in the first measure "hang" gets one beat, "down" gets two beats, and "your" gets one beat.

Now combine the notes to be played and the timing. Pluck the strings with your thumb.

Remember: When fretting the strings with the left hand, use finger 1 (pointer) for fret 1, finger 2 (social) for fret 2, finger 3 (ring) for fret 3, and finger 4 (pinky) for fret 4. Be sure to play (fret) this way from the start, since it will allow you to play songs more efficiently and faster as you gain experience.

EXERCISE—*Playing Melody Notes from Chords for "Tom Dooley"*

As a further exercise play the notes (melody) to "Tom Dooley" from the chord positions of the song. Change the structure of the chord only when necessary. For example, the first six measures are played with the G chord (that is, all open strings). The only time the G chord structure takes any change for the sake of the melody is the E note (fourth string, second fret) for the word "head." This E note added to the G chord is allowed for the necessity of playing the true melody of the song. Thus the G chord is distorted somewhat from its original form.

The next eight measures of the song are played with the D7 chord. The melody can be played from the D7 chord except for the notes of E and G ("head" and "Tom"). To play these melody notes, finger 2 on the third string, second fret can be lifted to hit the E note (fourth string, second fret) and remain lifted to play the G note (third string open).

This is what I call "distorting" the chord for the sake of the melody. It is extremely important to understand this technique. *Most melody notes of a song are found from the chord positions of that song or near them.*

Before going any further in this book, be sure you can do the following (practice!):

● Strum *chords* for "Tom Dooley," making each strum equal one whole beat.
● Play the *melody* notes for "Tom Dooley" with the right thumb, fretting with fingers of the left hand.
● Play the *melody* notes with respect to the chords of "Tom Dooley."

You should reach the point where you no longer need to look at the musical notation and can play "Tom Dooley" by "ear." Try it. *Practice.* Be patient and *think* of what you are doing. *All songs can be approached by this three-step method, so know it well.*

Tablature

There is another form of writing and reading music. It is called "tablature," tab for short.

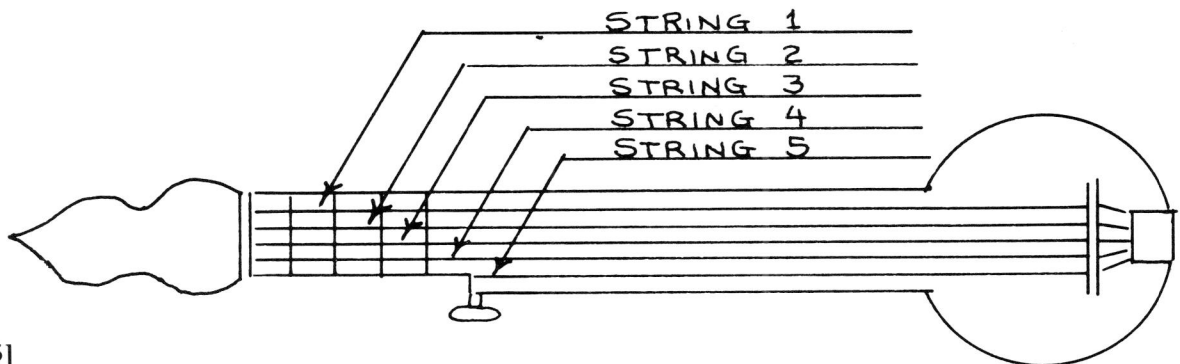

STRING 1
STRING 2
STRING 3
STRING 4
STRING 5

[Fig. 25]

Tab has five lines, but it is not to be confused with the treble clef's staff. If you set the banjo on your lap and looked down at it, it would look like Figure 25. This sequence of strings is the same as the lines in tablature. The top line represents string 1, the bottom line represents string 5. See the tab staff in Figure 26.

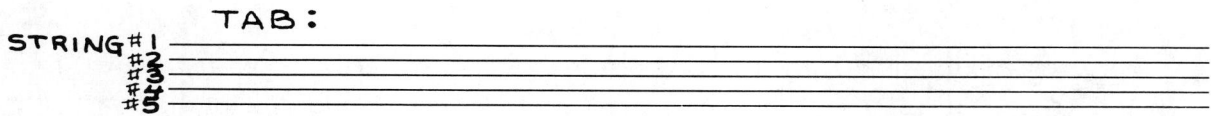

TAB:

STRING #1
#2
#3
#4
#5

[Fig. 26]

Let's take another look at the scale of G major. As a review, play the scale in Figure 27. (*Remember:* G = do, and so on.)

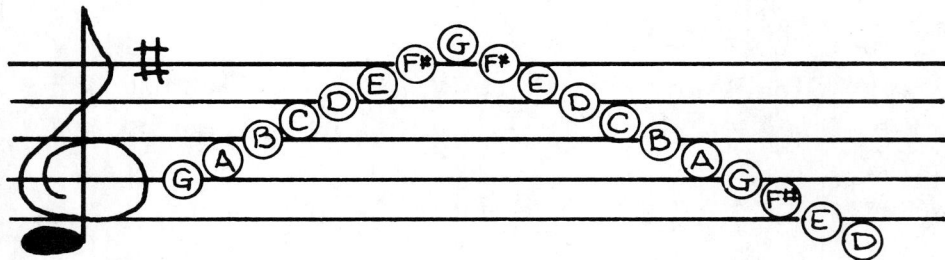

[Fig. 27]

In tab form, the scale of G major looks like Figure 28. Tablature is read from left to right. The number on the tab indicates what fret to press on that particular string. For example, a 1 means first fret, 2 is the second fret, 3 is the third fret, 4 is the fourth fret, and a 0 means the string is played "open" (or zero fret). (Remember which fingers to use? Finger 1 for fret 1, and so on.)

TAB:

STRING #1
#2
#3
#4
#5

0 2 0 1 0 2 4 4 2 0 1 0 2 0 4 2 0
0
G A B C D E F# G F# E D C B A G F# E D

[Fig. 28]

In other words, the G note is played on the third string open (0), the A note is played on the third string, second fret (2), the B note is played on the second string open (0), and so on.

24

Now let's take the scale of G major again and play the same notes on a few different strings, as in Figure 29.

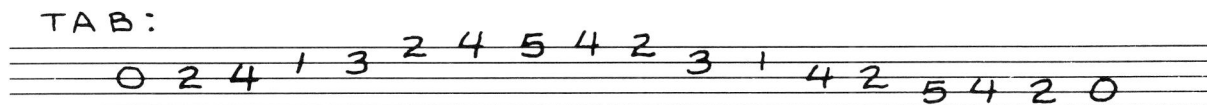

```
TAB:
                          2   4   5   4   2
          0   2   4   1   3               3   1
                                                  4   2
                                                      5   4   2   0
```

[Fig. 29]

Do you see the difference between this and the scale you just played? Are the notes still the same? What about the location of the notes with respect to the strings and frets?

EXERCISE—*Writing the Scale of G in Tab Form*

Write in Figure 30 the notes from G to G′ (octave higher) back to G again for the notes in the scale of G major (that is, G, A, B, C, D, E, F#, G, F#, E, D, C, B, A, G) in tab form on the third string only. (See answer at Fig. 30A.) This proportion will be a key to understanding the "major diatonic scale" explained next.

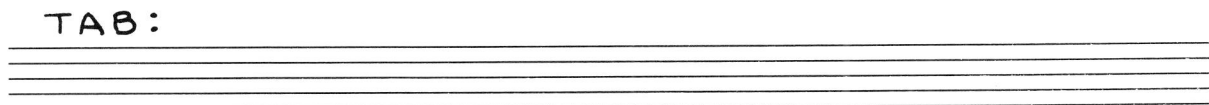

```
TAB:
```

[Fig. 30]

Answer to exercise:

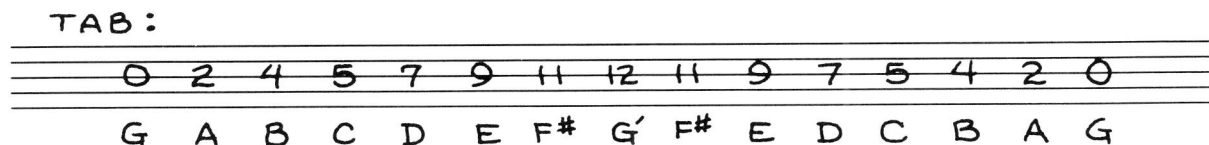

```
TAB:
       0   2   4   5   7   9   11   12   11   9   7   5   4   2   0

       G   A   B   C   D   E   F#   G′   F#   E   D   C   B   A   G
```

[Fig. 30A]

25

The Major Diatonic Scale

The major diatonic scale is the most common scale used in music. It is the one we learned as kids (remember do, re, mi?). There is a definite proportion to the notes of do, re, mi, fa, sol, la, ti, do. Sing it to yourself. No matter what note you start on, the proportion from "do" to "do" remains the same.

Whatever note "do" is indicates the key. For example, if the "do" note is G, you're in the key of G; if the "do" note is C, you're in the key of C, and so on. But the proportions between these eight tones are still the same, no matter what key you're in!

Let's take a second look at the tablature exercise you just completed. As a review, play the notes (scale) again (Fig. 31). What you have just played is the "major diatonic scale" for the key of G major as played on the third string.

[Fig. 31]

Question: Is the F# necessary? Try playing the scale with the "ti" note being F rather than F# (Fig. 32).

[Fig. 32]

It sounds strange. Right? Where is the clinker? Play it again. The unwelcome note is F. Now play the scale using the F# instead of the F (Fig. 33).

[Fig. 33]

26

Much better! That is what we are accustomed to hearing. (Who says we are not products of our environment and our culture?) That sequence of notes is called the major diatonic scale. ''Major'' because it sounds more dominant to us than ''minor.'' ''Diatonic'' because it is made up of ''dia-tones''; that is, the scale is played ''through'' the twelve half-step notes shown in Figure 34A. ''Scale'' is left to the reader to look up in Webster.

Figure 34A shows the proportions for the notes in the major diatonic scale for the key of G on the third string (G). Figure 34B is the same scale as it would appear on the treble clef. Let's analyze this scale. If the major diatonic scale is defined by the proportion of notes, what is true for the key of G should also be true for the major diatonic scales of the other keys.

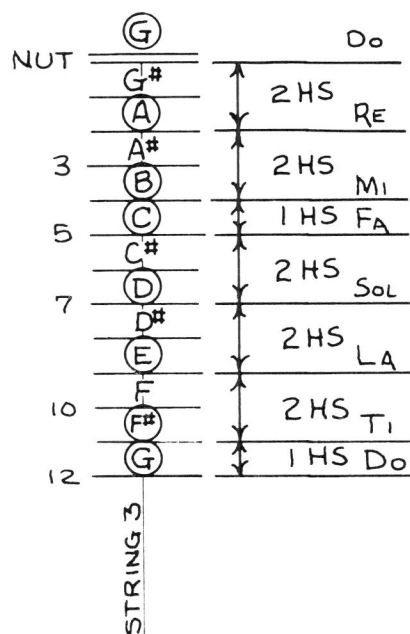

[Fig. 34A]

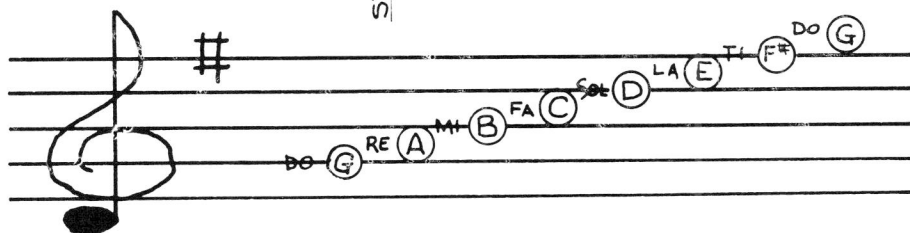

[Fig. 34B]

Look again at the notes in the major diatonic scale for the key of G as they are located on the third string of the banjo (Fig. 34A). Keep in mind that going up one fret equals going up one half step (HS): from ''do'' to ''re'' is two frets or two HS, from ''re'' to ''mi'' is another two HS, from ''mi'' to ''fa'' is one HS, from ''fa'' to ''sol'' is two HS, from ''sol'' to ''la'' is two HS, from ''la'' to ''ti'' is two HS, and from ''ti'' to ''do'' is one HS.

There is indeed a sequence. From ''do'' to ''do'' the half-step ratio is 2, 2, 1, jump 2 HS, then repeat the HS sequence of 2, 2, and 1.

From the chromatic circle cycle (CCC) we can now derive a formula! Let the low ''do'' note (G, third string open) be assigned the number 1. Go around the CCC clockwise. Each adjacent HS is the next number in the sequence (that is, G# = 2, A = 3, A# = 4, B = 5, and so on). (See Fig. 35.)

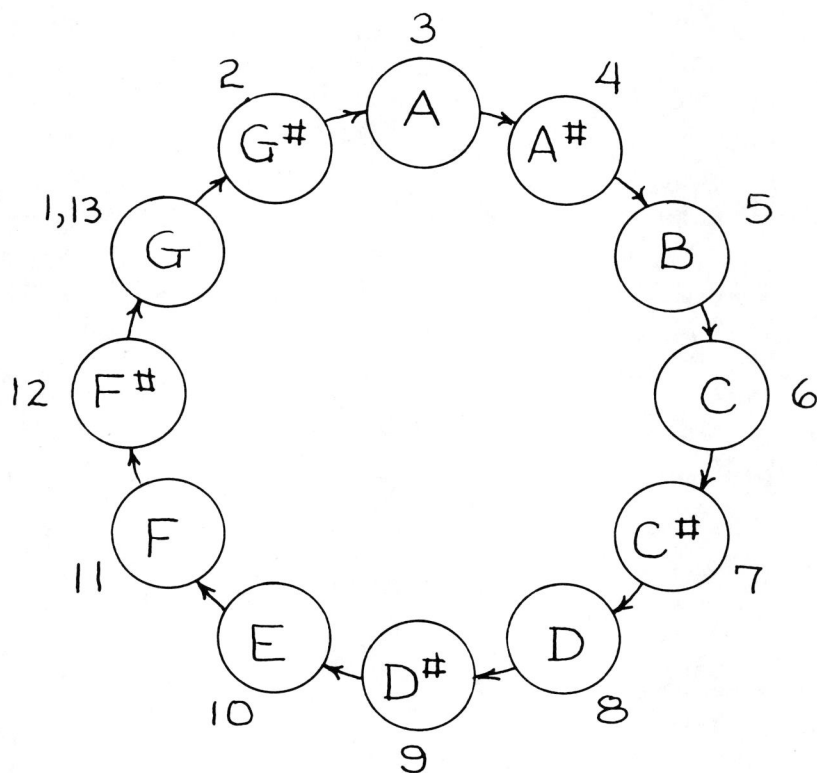

[Fig. 35]

Here then is the derived proportion (formula) for the major diatonic scale of G major:

1	3	5	6	8	10	12	13
G	A	B	C	D	E	F#	G
do	re	mi	fa	sol	la	ti	do

The number 13 is the same as 1 because the CCC has a "modulus of 12" just like our clock. That is the same as 1 P.M. being 13 o'clock! Right?

I call the key of G major "people's key number one." *It is important to know the key of G well, inside and out.* Ninety percent of all bluegrass songs I know are in the key of G. If a song is in another key, all you need is a capo to move up or down the neck. More on the capo and transposing later.

"People's key number two" is the key of C major. It is probably the second most common key used in folk music. (*Question:* Isn't all music "folk?" To quote an old-timer, "I ain't never heard *horses* sing.")

For the key of C the major diatonic scale by deductive reasoning must be in the proportion of 1, 3, 5, 6, 8, 10, 12, 13 with the number 1 note being C, that is, the "do" note for the key of C. Going around the CCC clockwise again with C being 1, we come up with the following scale for the key of C:

1	3	5	6	8	10	12	13
C	D	E	F	G	A	B	C

28

Play the notes of the scale, as shown in Figure 36. Sounds right to our ears, doesn't it? If this proportion works for the keys of G and C, then it becomes intuitively obvious to the most casual observer that it will work for any other major key.

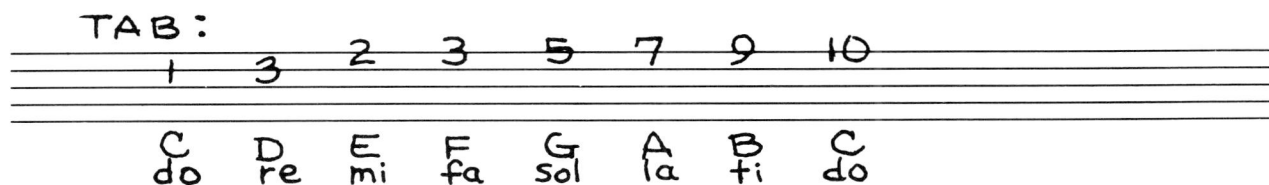

[Fig. 36]

Go back and play the scale for the key of G (Fig. 27). What is the difference between the two scales? *Answer:* The scale of C is exactly five half steps higher than the scale of G. Prove it to yourself by comparing the CCC for both keys.

EXERCISE—*Deriving Notes for Various Keys*

With the proportion of 1, 3, 5, 6, 8, 10, 12, 13, derive the notes in the major diatonic scale from the CCC for the keys of A, D, and E. Write them in the spaces provided in Figure 37. Keep in mind the "do" note is the number 1 note of that particular key.

	1 do	3 re	5 mi	6 fa	8 sol	10 la	12 ti	13 do
Key of G	G	A	B	C	D	E	F#	G
Key of C	C	D	E	F	G	A	B	C
Key of A								
Key of D								
Key of E								

[Fig. 37]

Answer to exercise: A: A, B, C#, D, E, F#, G#, A
D: D, E, F#, G, A, B, C#, D
E: E, F#, G#, A, B, C#, D#, E

29

EXERCISE—*Making a Template*

An easy method for using the proportions described in this book is to make a template for the major diatonic scale. Here is how to do it (see Fig. 38):

● Lay a transparent sheet of paper over the CCC in Figure 4.

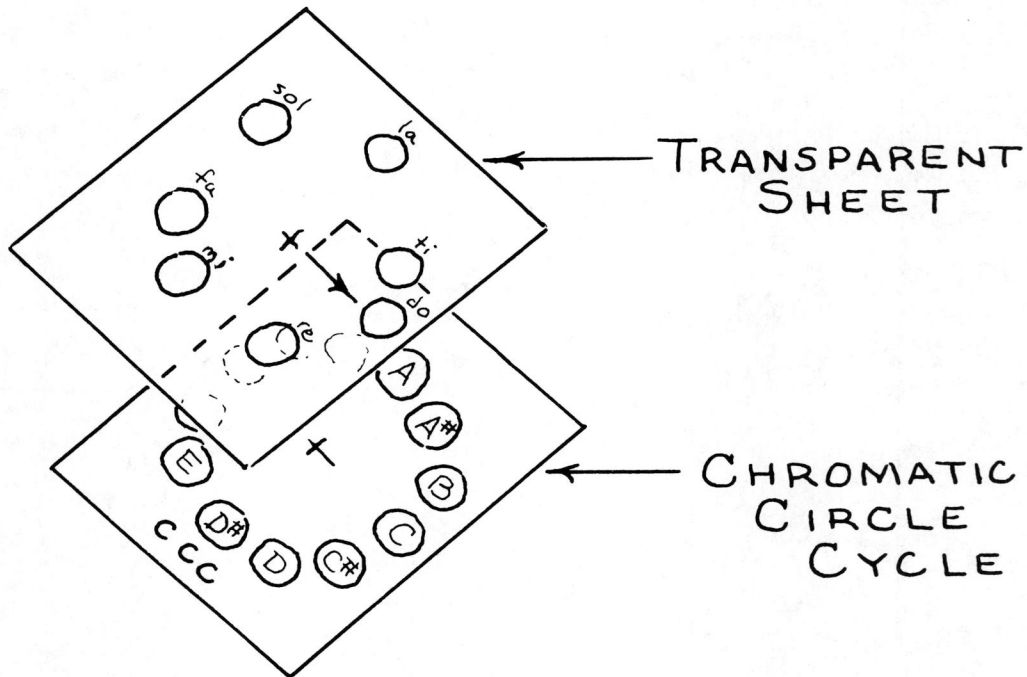

[Fig. 38]

● Mark the center of the CCC with a cross.
● Circle all the notes in the major diatonic scale for the key of C: C, D, E, F, G, A, B.
● Draw an arrow from the center to note C and write "root note (do) for major diatonic scale." The result is provided for you in Figure 39.
● Label all the tones (C = do, D = re, E = mi, etc.) outside the note circles drawn.
● Make a copy of the CCC from Figure 4 in a similar manner and transfer both this and the template to cardboard for more usability and permanence.
● Place the template over the CCC, aligning the centers and fastening with a pronged clip. Now you can rotate the template to whatever key desired. The arrow points to the "do" note indicating the key.

LA

10

SOL

8

TI

12

DO

+   ROOT NOTE (DO)
      ————————————→
         FOR
      MAJOR DIATONIC
         SCALE

1, 13

FA

6

MI

5

RE

3

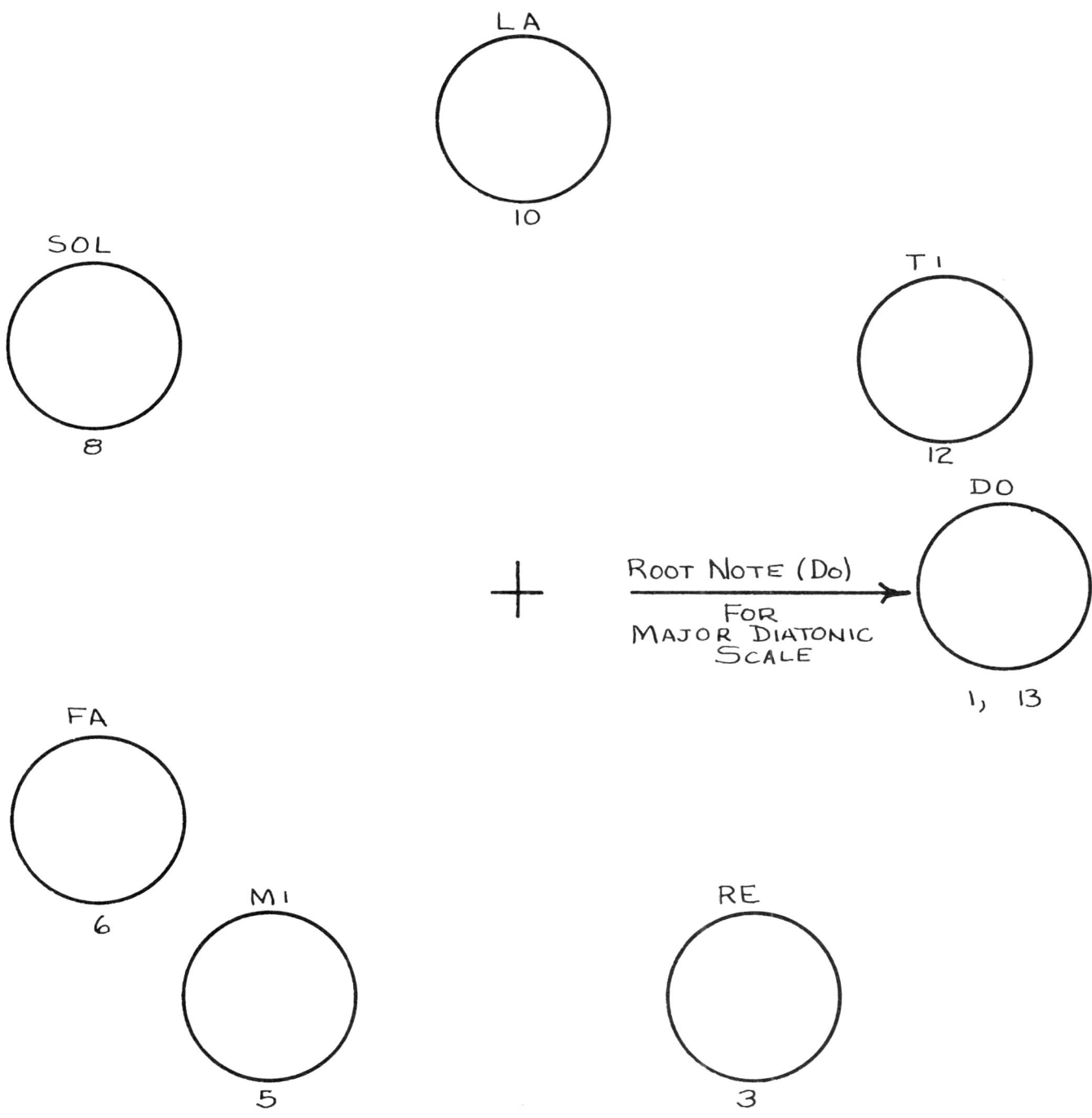

[Fig. 39.   Template for the major diatonic scale]

31

EXERCISE—*Writing the Scale for All Keys*

Fill in Figure 40. Use sharps (#) for the keys of G, D, A, E, and B. Use flats (♭) for the keys of F, B♭, E♭, A♭, D♭, and G♭. See Figure 41 for the answer.

Key of	do	re	mi	fa	sol	la	ti	do
C								
G								
D								
A								
E								
B								
F								
B♭								
E♭								
A♭								
D♭								
G♭								

[Fig. 40]

Answer to exercise:

Key of	do	re	mi	fa	sol	la	ti	do
C	C	D	E	F	G	A	B	C
G	G	A	B	C	D	E	F$^{\#}$	G
D	D	E	F$^{\#}$	G	A	B	C$^{\#}$	D
A	A	B	C$^{\#}$	D	E	F$^{\#}$	G$^{\#}$	A
E	E	F$^{\#}$	G$^{\#}$	A	B	C$^{\#}$	D$^{\#}$	E
B	B	C$^{\#}$	D$^{\#}$	E	F$^{\#}$	G$^{\#}$	A$^{\#}$	B
F	F	G	A	B^{b}	C	D	E	F
B^{b}	B^{b}	C	D	E^{b}	F	G	A	B^{b}
E^{b}	E^{b}	F	G	A^{b}	B^{b}	C	D	E^{b}
A^{b}	A^{b}	B^{b}	C	D^{b}	E^{b}	F	G	A^{b}
D^{b}	D^{b}	E^{b}	F	G^{b}	A^{b}	B^{b}	C	D^{b}
G^{b}	G^{b}	A^{b}	B^{b}	B (C^{b}) D^{b}	E^{b}	F	G^{b}

[Fig. 41]

You now have the major diatonic scale for every key possible. These will be the notes played (99 percent of the time) for each major key. To put aside any doubts you may have, look up any song in any major key in any music book and see for yourself.

THE TWELVE MAJOR KEY SIGNATURES

By knowing the notes for the scales of each major key, it stands to reason that you can now write the "key signature" for each of the twelve major keys (see Fig. 42).

Figure 42 can also be used as a reference to find the key for any song you are interested in. For example, if you have a song with three sharps, you can easily see from the figure that it is in the key of A.

Here are some points to keep in mind:

● The key of G has only one sharp—F$^{\#}$.
● The key of C has no sharps or flats.
● The sharp key signatures can be determined by noting the last sharp written (from left to right); then by going up one half step, you find the name of the key. For example, in the key of E the sharps are F$^{\#}$, C$^{\#}$, G$^{\#}$, and D$^{\#}$. One half step above D$^{\#}$ is E—the key name.
● The flat key signatures with two or more flats can be determined by the second from the last flat. For example, the key of A^{b} has flats (from left to right) of B^{b}, E^{b}, A^{b}, and D^{b}. The second from the last flat is A^{b}—the key name.
● The key of F has one flat—B^{b}.

[Fig. 42]

Double-thumbing

Now let's make your playing a little trickier and try "double-thumbing." When you use this technique, every other note played is the first string plucked by finger 2, and every note between those notes is plucked by the thumb. The thumb will alternate between the second, third, or fourth string and the fifth string, thus the name "double-thumbing." Note that the thumb never will pluck the first string. The basic double-thumbing pattern is shown in Figure 43.

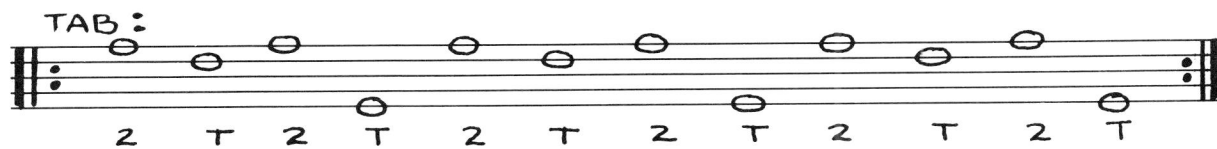

[Fig. 43]

The number and letter below the tablature indicates which finger of the right hand plucks which string when. For example, finger 2 plucks the first string open, then the thumb plucks the second string open. (The dots at either end of the measure are "repeat" signs. That is, when you are playing a song and come to these dots, repeat all the notes in that measure before moving on to the next.) *Repeat the basic double-thumbing pattern until it becomes second nature to you.*

It is important to move your thumb at free will (with control) from one string to the next, since your thumb will be playing the song melody. The following exercises illustrate the technique of double-thumbing with a "floating thumb." In the double-thumbing pattern,

35

rather than playing the second string only for every other thumb beat (Fig. 43), that beat can now be played on the second, third, or fourth string; thus the thumb "floats" from string to string. Try it for yourself!

EXERCISE—*Double-thumbing with Floating Thumb for Chords in the Key of G*

Let's start with the G major chord (Fig. 44).

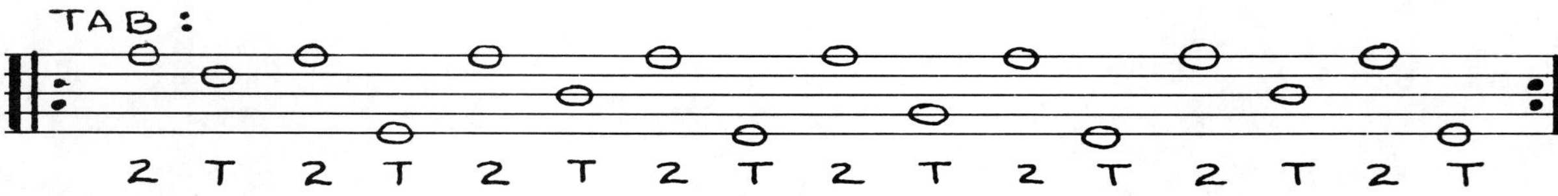

TAB:

2 T 2 T 2 T 2 T 2 T 2 T 2 T 2 T 2 T

[Fig. 44]

When you have mastered the G major chord, try playing the D7 chord (Fig. 45).

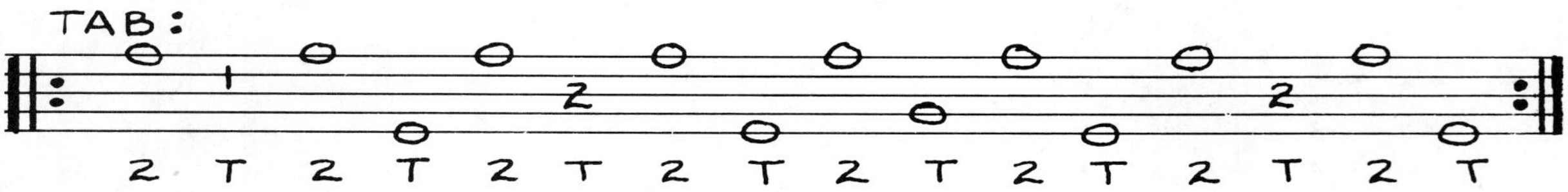

TAB:

2 T 2 T 2 T 2 T 2 T 2 T 2 T 2 T

[Fig. 45]

Now fill in the blank tablature (Fig. 46) for double-thumbing with a floating thumb for the chord of C major. (See Fig. 47 for the answer.)

TAB:

[Fig. 46]

Answer to exercise:

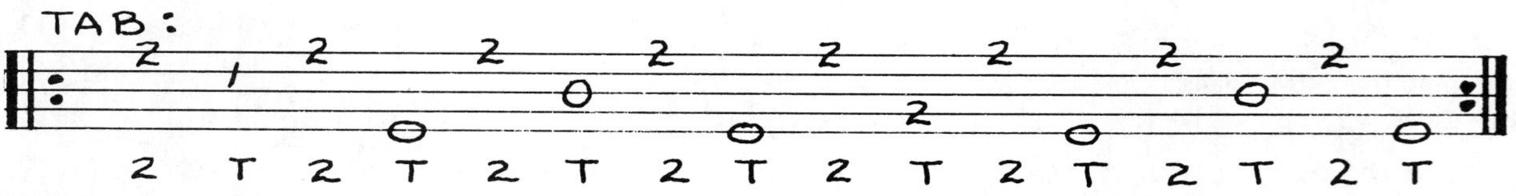

TAB:

2 T 2 T 2 T 2 T 2 T 2 T 2 T 2 T

[Fig. 47]

EXERCISE—*Playing in the Key of G with Double-thumbing*

Now that you have the hang of double-thumbing, try playing the songs on pages 12–14 again, using the double-thumbing technique.

Practice double-thumbing until you get to the point where you no longer have to look at your right-hand fingers to see what they are doing. If you have to look, it will only slow you down because of the time it takes to go from mind to finger back to mind again (Fig. 48).

[Fig. 48]

This is the time to develop your personal flare for the song being played. When you get to the second-nature point of double-thumbing, you can "feel" the song you are playing. That is, you can add accents and rhythms and use your instincts as to how you feel the song should be. But before you get to this point, you must log many an hour on mastering the fundamentals. *Practice, practice, practice!*

Keep the right hand double-thumbing no matter what the left hand wants to do, just as in the simple strum. Above everything else, the rhythm must be steady, not spasmodic. If the left hand wants to slow you down, it means you need more practice making and changing chords. Keep the right hand going only as fast or as slowly as the left hand will allow in changing chords.

EXERCISE—*Double-thumbing "Tom Dooley"*

Refer to the song "Tom Dooley" in Figures 24 and 49. First, assign the number of beats in double-thumbing to each note. This song has quarter, half, and whole notes. To keep a decent pace to the song, I made one complete double-thumbing cycle (four beats—T-2-T-2) equivalent to a half note. Therefore, by proportions the quarter note must get two beats of the double-thumbing cycle (T-2). *Question:* How many beats does the whole note get?

37

Answer: The whole note is twice as long as the half note; therefore, it gets eight beats or two whole double-thumbing cycles—T-2-T-2-T-2-T-2.

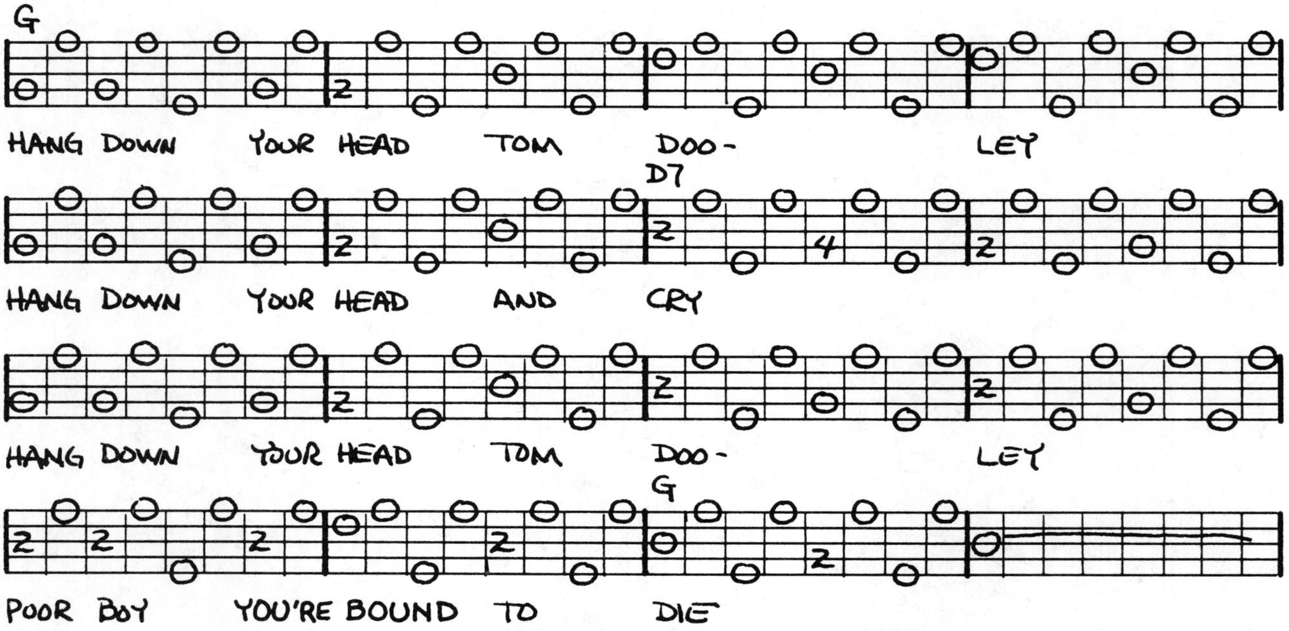

HANG DOWN   YOUR HEAD   TOM   DOO-   LEY

HANG DOWN   YOUR HEAD   AND   CRY

HANG DOWN   YOUR HEAD   TOM   DOO-   LEY

POOR BOY   YOU'RE BOUND   TO   DIE

[Fig. 49]

In measure 1 of Figure 49 the D notes are located on the fourth string open. In measure 2 "head" is an E note. This is played by finger 2 on the second fret of the fourth string. (Here and in other measures the number given is the fret number.)

Measures 1 and 2 are the same as measures 5 and 6 and measures 9 and 10. This repetition makes the song easier to learn.

In measure 3 "Doo" is a whole note (eight beats long) played on the second string open (B). Since the B note has to be sustained for eight beats because it is the melody of the song, it is plucked a little harder than the rest of the seven beats. When the thumb goes to hit the fifth beat of the measure, be sure it does not play the note that is being sustained (B note, second string open) since that could confuse the melody. Instead, that fifth beat is played "around" the melody note, usually part of the chord being played at the time. In this case, the fifth beat is the third string open (G note), which is part of the G chord played during the first six measures of the song.

Measure 4 is played the same as measure 3, since "ley" is a B note sustained for eight beats.

At measure 7 the song changes chords. It goes from a G major chord (all strings played open) to a D7 chord.

Here is the key (trick?) to 99 percent of all songs and arrangements I know:

- Always play the melody.
- Keep it clean and well timed.
- Play the melody around the chords of the song.
- Alter the chord to fit the melody if necessary.
- But by all means keep the melody clear.

In measure 2 the E note was played for "head." Here we deviate a little from the open-G chord, but that is all right since it will blend in by being part of the major diatonic scale for the key of G.

At measures 7 and 8 "cry" is held (the A note is already part of the D7 chord) for two whole notes. That is sixteen beats the A note is to be sustained. To keep the song from being monotonous by either playing the A note every fourth beat or hitting the fourth string open every fourth beat, a little "run" is used. Figure 50 shows a common run for the D7 chord.

[Fig. 50]

The F# is fretted by finger 4, and the E note is fretted by finger 2. Finger 2 is removed from string 3 on the second fret and is placed on string 4 of the second fret to make the E note. Remember, it is all right to change the chord slightly, but not to alter the melody. Note also that this run of A, F#, E, and D are all part of the major diatonic scale of the key of G.

Measures 7 to 14 are played with the D7 chord for the song, so keep the left hand making that chord. Alter the chord only when necessary for the melody. The only time the D7 chord is changed is at the beginning of measure 8 to play the F# and E notes for the run, at the beginning of measure 10 finger 2 is moved to play the E note, and finally, at the beginning of measure 14 finger 1 is lifted to play the B note for "bound." At all other times the fingers are playing the D7 chord.

At measure 15 the song goes back to the chord of G. Usually a song will end in the chord that is the same name of the key (in this case, G).

Note also that the song ends on a G note. In the last measure, the G note is held for eight counts. A rule of thumb is that the last note played in a song is the same as the key of the song (in this case, G).

EXERCISE—*Double-thumbing "Bingo"*

Now that you have gone through "Tom Dooley" with double-thumbing, try double-thumbing "Bingo" by yourself (Fig. 51). To write the tablature for double-thumbing "Bingo," go through the same procedure as we did in double-thumbing "Tom Dooley":

[Fig. 51]

- Play the chords of the song first, humming the melody as you go along.
- Play the melody alone. The song is in 2/4 time. That means the quarter note gets a whole beat, and there are two whole beats (quarter notes) to the measure. However, there are many eighth notes in this song. As in math, $1/4 = 2 \times 1/8$; the eighth note gets half of a whole beat. The second measure is the first full measure of the song and would be counted as "one-and-two-and." In other words, "one-and" is a whole beat (two eighth notes equals one quarter note), as is "two-and."

  Since the song is in 2/4 time, there is the possibility of the following combinations: two quarter notes to the measure ($2 \times 1/4 = 2/4$), as in measure 5; four eighth notes to the measure ($4 \times 1/8 = 4/8 = 2/4$), as in measure 2; or two eighth notes and one quarter note to the measure ($2 \times 1/8 + 1/4 = 2/8 + 1/4 = 1/4 + 1/4 = 2/4$), as in measure 7.
- Play the melody with respect to the chords. There are three chords to "Bingo" (G, C, and D7). Remember that it is all right to distort the chord somewhat for the sake of the melody.
- Now fill in the tablature for double-thumbing "Bingo" (Fig 52). At this point, each note must be assigned so many beats of double-thumbing (T-2-T-2). To keep this song moving at a decent pace, I assigned each eighth note two double-thumb beats (T-2). (When you finish, compare with the answer in Fig. 53.)

Each measure of tablature has eight vertical spaces; therefore, each vertical space is equivalent to a sixteenth note. Two vertical spaces are the time for an eighth note and four vertical spaces for a quarter note. In this example, then, each measure of tab is equivalent to a measure of the song "Bingo." This proof is left to the student.

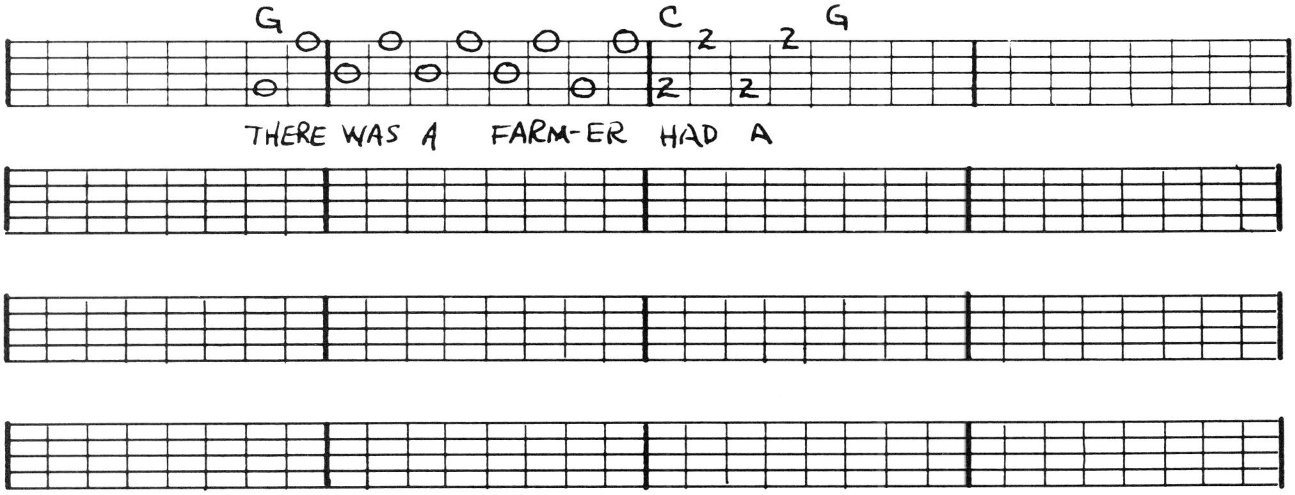

[Fig. 52]

G   C   G

THERE WAS A FARM-ER HAD A

[Fig. 52]

Answer to exercise:

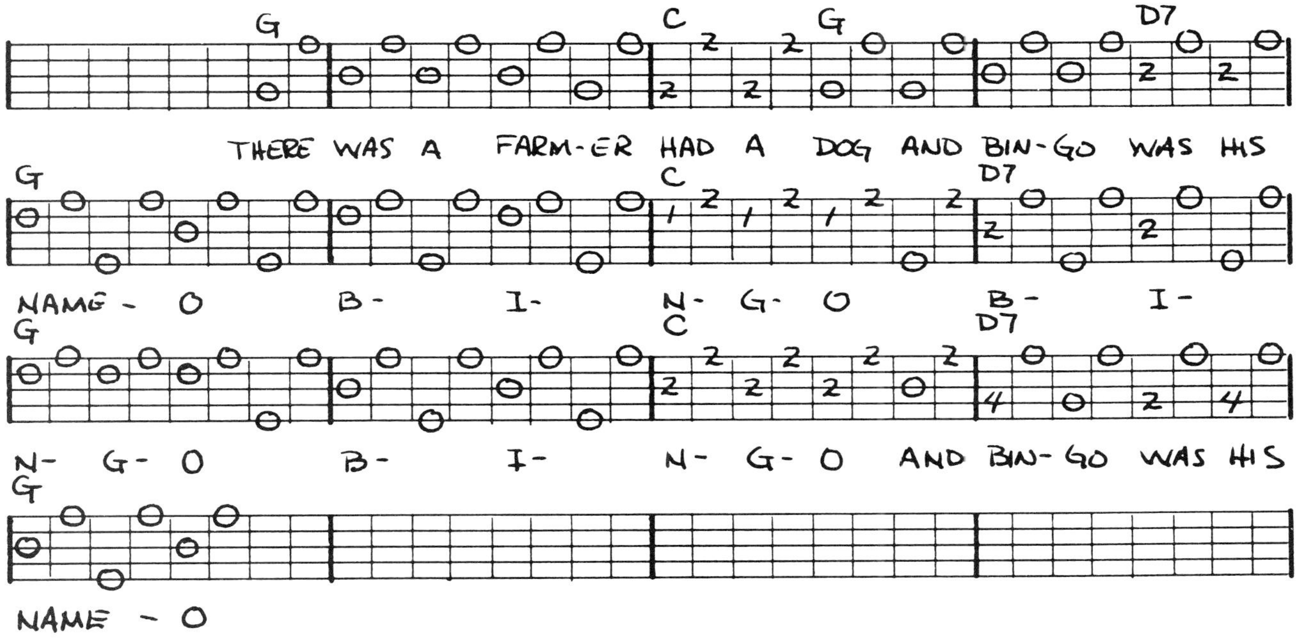

G   C   G   D7

THERE WAS A FARM-ER HAD A DOG AND BIN-GO WAS HIS

G   C   D7

NAME - O   B-   I-   N- G- O   B-   I-

G   C   D7

N- G- O   B-   I-   N- G- O AND BIN-GO WAS HIS

G

NAME - O

[Fig. 53]

Since there is only one sharp in "Bingo" ($F\sharp$), it is in the key of G. Note also that the song starts in the G major chord and ends in it. Again, the last note of the song is a G note. All these signs indicate what key the song is in.

The first measure has only one eighth note. This is not a full measure of 2/4. The last measure of the song makes up the difference of the first measure to make a completed 2/4 measure. That is, the first measure = 1/8 note, the last measure = 1/4 note + 1/8 note, and the first and last measure combined = 1/8 + 1/4 + 1/8 = 2/8 + 1/4 = 1/4 + 1/4 = 2/4. Whenever any song is incomplete in the first measure, the last measure when combined with the first will add up to the sum of the time signature.

Chords

It has already been illustrated that music has mathematical proportions. Here is more proof. Let's analyze the G major chord (Fig. 54).

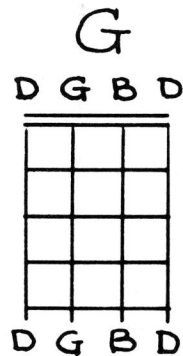

G

D G B D

[Fig. 54]　　　　　D G B D ◄——————— Notes played
for G major chord

The banjo is tuned to open G. That is, all the strings played open make a G major chord. The actual notes played (from the fifth to the first string) are G, D, G, B, and D. Notice there are only three different notes being played—G, B, and D. Assign to the root note the number 1. The root note in this case is G, since the G chord is being played. This is the same technique we used to find the root note for the major diatonic scale.

Going clockwise on the Chromatic Circle Cycle (Fig. 4), G is note 1, B is note 5, and D is note 8. The proportion for the G major chord is 1, 5, 8.

Is this 1, 5, 8 combination true for all major chords? Let's analyze the C major chord (Fig. 55).

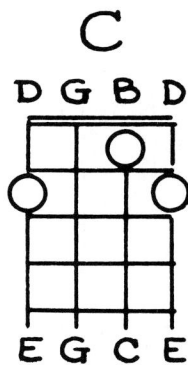

C

D G B D

[Fig. 55]　　　　　E G C E ◄——————— Notes played
for C major chord

The notes for this chord are two Es, a G, and a C. Since this is a C major chord, the root note is C. Now start with the C note being note 1, and go around the CCC (Fig. 4) in a clockwise direction. The next note in this sequence is E, and then G. The notes in the C major chord have a sequence of C, E, G. This proportion is 1, 5, 8!

We now have a formula for finding any major chord. It is 1, 5, 8.

To make a "seventh" chord, you would keep the ratio of the major chord and add to it an extra note three half steps higher than note 8. The ratio for a seventh chord would be 1, 5, 8, 11. Let's take the D7 chord as an example (Fig. 56). The notes played for the D7 chord, in sequence starting with the root note D, are D, F#, A, and C, which have the ratio of 1, 5, 8, 11.

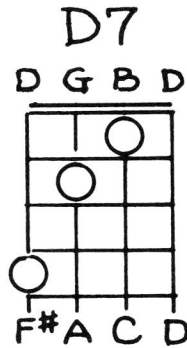

D7

D G B D

[Fig. 56]   F# A C D ◄————————— Notes played
                                        for D7 chord

To make a minor chord, the second note of the major chord must be lowered a half step. We would then have the ratio of 1, 4, 8. Take the E minor (Em) chord as an example (Fig. 57). With E being the root note 1, the notes played for Em are E, G, and B, which have the ratio of 1, 4, 8.

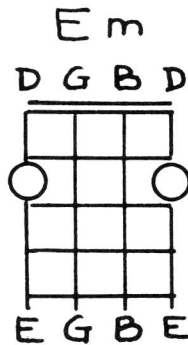

Em

D G B D

[Fig. 57]   E G B E ◄————————— Notes played
                                       for Em chord

CHORD FORMULAS

So far the following chord formulas have been derived:

● Major chord = 1, 5, 8
● Seventh chord = 1, 5, 8, 11
● Minor chord = 1, 4, 8

Other formulas for various types of chords are as follows:

● Minor seventh chord = 1, 4, 8, 11
● Major seventh chord = 1, 5, 8, 12

- Sixth chord = 1, 5, 8, 10
- Ninth chord = 1, 3, 5, 8, 11
- Augmented chord = 1, 5, 9
- Diminished chord = 1, 4, 7, 10

These are all ratios of half steps counting clockwise from note 1. Note 1 is always the root note; that is, note 1 for B7 is B, note 1 for the Am chord is A, and so on.

EXERCISE—*Making a Template*

Rather than counting the notes out each time for a chord, a key (template) can be made for each type of chord and layed over the CCC. Use the same procedure as for making a template to find the notes in the major diatonic scale.

For example, a major chord has the half-step proportion of 1, 5, 8. Simply make a template with cut-out circles for the proportions of 1, 5, 8 from the CCC (Fig. 4), drawing an arrow from the center to the root note 1 and labeling the template "major chord" (Fig. 58).

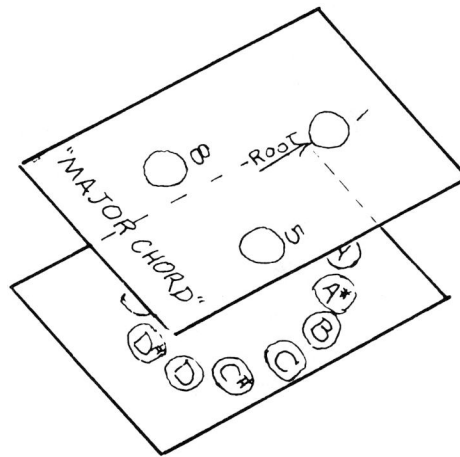

[Fig. 58]

Now all you have to do to find the notes in the chord is to fasten the template to a copy of the CCC and dial in the root note for that particular chord.

CREATING CHORDS

To make a chord, all notes in the formula must be played together at least once. It is all right to play the same note more than once, but all the notes to make that chord must be played. The sequence of the notes doesn't have to be in order of the ratio.

Let's take the C major chord as an example. The proportion for a major chord is 1, 5, 8; therefore, the notes for C major must be C, E, G. That means C, E, and G must be played at least once.

Now let's take one string at a time to create a C major chord. The fourth string open is a D note. Go up the neck until the first note is found for the C major chord—either a C, E, or

G. An E note is found on the D string at the second fret. The third string open is a G, part of the C major chord, so don't fret it. The second string open is a B note, one fret up is a C note. Finally the first string is a D note open and two frets up is an E note (just like the fourth string, right?). The notes now being played from the fourth string to the first string are E, G, C, E—a form of the C major chord (Fig. 59). The playing of the E, G, C notes is called an "inversion" which means not the exact C, E, G sequence for the C major chord.

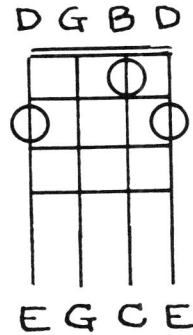

D G B D

[Fig. 59]

E G C E

EXERCISE—*Banjo Chords with Open-G Tuning*

Fill out the chord blanks in Figure 60 from the following chord formulas:

- Major chords (G, C, D, A, E, F) = 1, 5, 8
- Seventh chords (D7, G7, C7, A7, B7) = 1, 5, 8, 11
- Minor chords (Am, Dm, Em, Fm) = 1, 4, 8

The G major chord is symbolized simply by G, the A minor chord by Am. Answers are given in Figure 61. The tie line in Figure 61 (in A, A7, B7, Fm) between two locations on a fret indicates that one finger (usually finger 1) should press across all four strings at that fret. The circled numbers in the diagram indicate the left-hand finger locations.

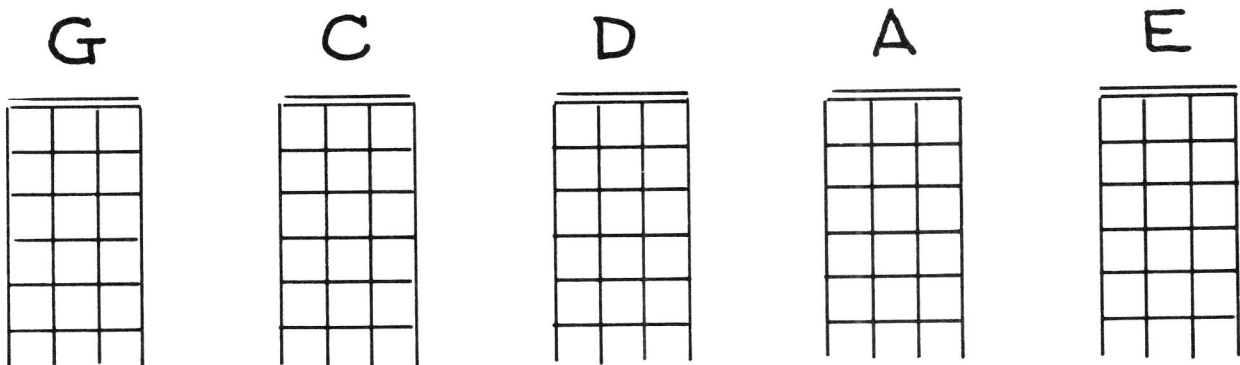

G   C   D   A   E

[Fig. 60]

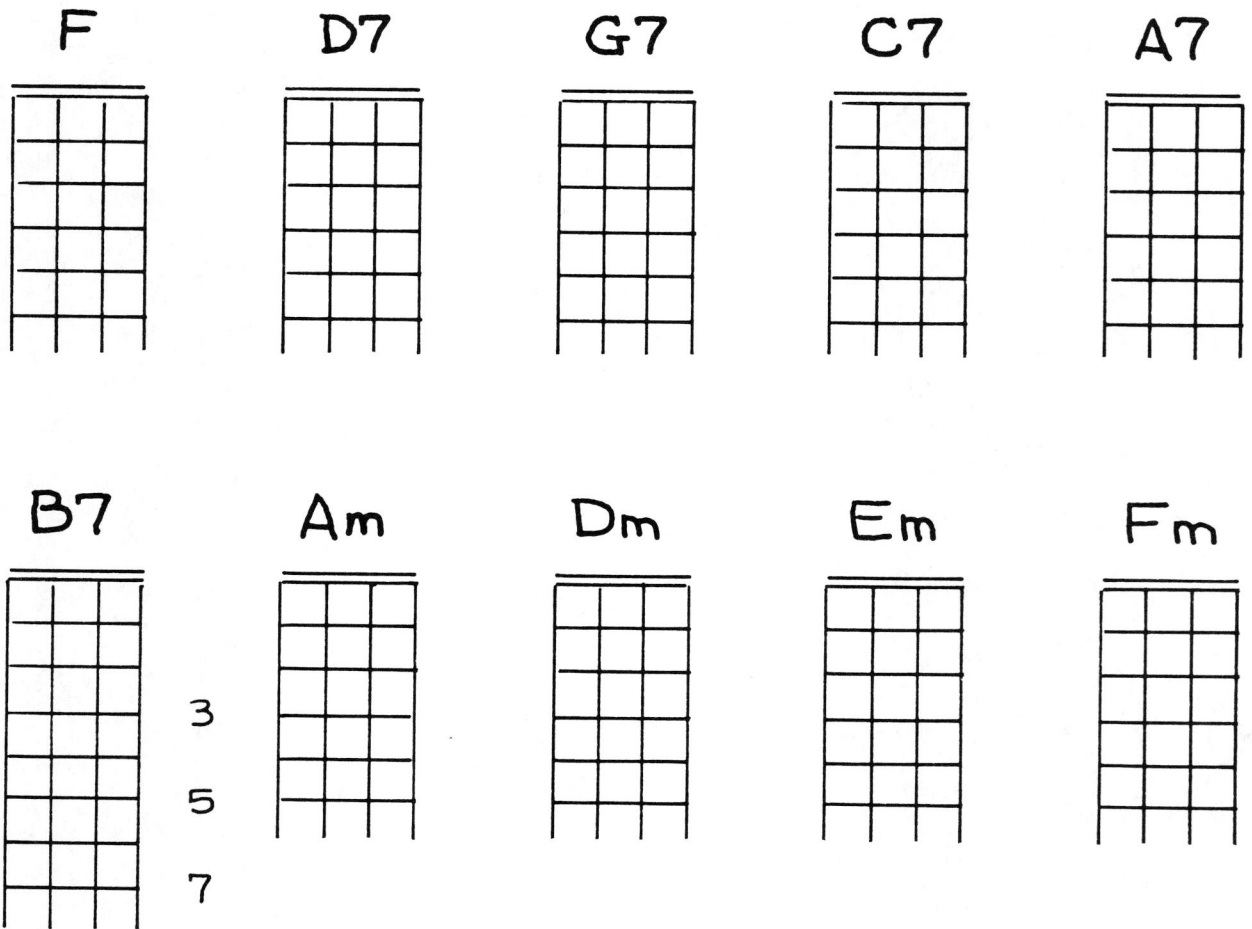

F   **D7**   **G7**   **C7**   **A7**

5

B7   **Am**   **Dm**   **Em**   **Fm**

3

5

7

[Fig. 60. Cont.]

Answer to exercise:

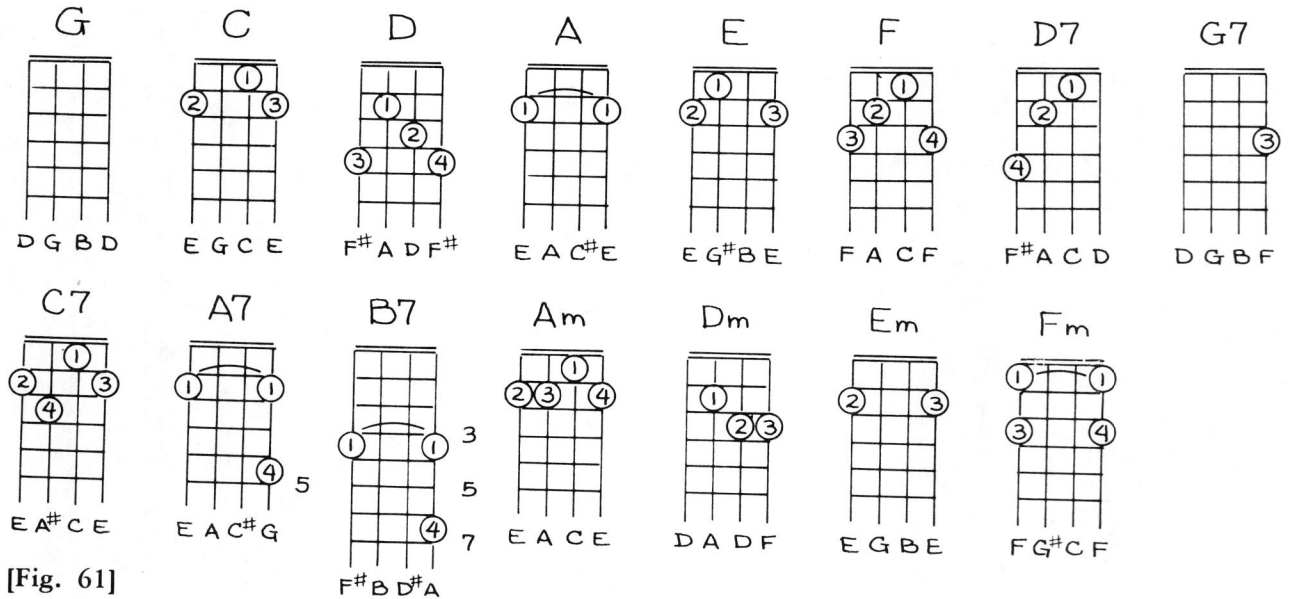

G   **C**   **D**   **A**   **E**   **F**   **D7**   **G7**

D G B D   E G C E   F♯ A D F♯   E A C♯ E   E G♯ B E   F A C F   F♯ A C D   D G B F

C7   **A7**   **B7**   **Am**   **Dm**   **Em**   **Fm**

3

5

5

7

E A♯ C E   E A C♯ G   F♯ B D♯ A   E A C E   D A D F   E G B E   F G♯ C F

[Fig. 61]

46

BAR CHORDS

It is important for you to know the chords of G, D, F, G7, Am, and Fm well. They are basic chords that are fretted on all four strings. Because of this, you can form new chords from them by moving up and down the neck.

Going "up the neck" means moving the left-hand fingering toward the bridge, thus making the strings shorter and therefore raising the pitch. Going "down the neck" is just the opposite, thus the left-hand fingering moves away from the bridge, lengthening the strings and therefore lowering the notes.

As an example, make an F major chord (Fig. 62A). Now, keeping your left-hand fingers in the same relative position, go up the neck by one whole fret. This new chord becomes an F# major chord (Fig. 62B). Go up one more fret in this F position. You now have a G major chord (Fig. 62C). Can you prove it? *Hint:* What notes are actually being played?

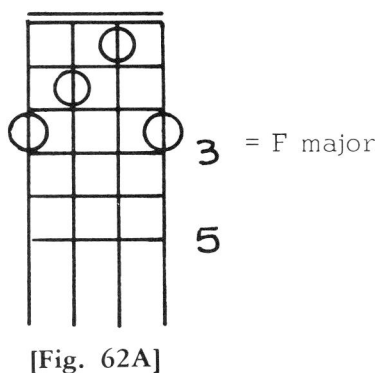

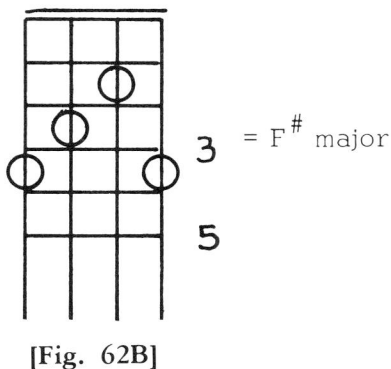

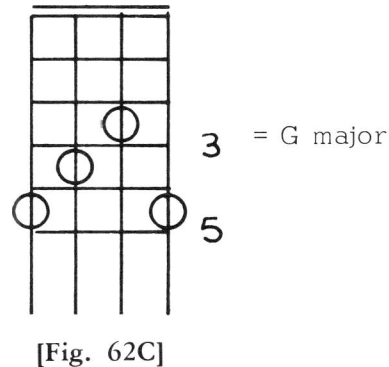

| [Fig. 62A] | [Fig. 62B] | [Fig. 62C] |

Each note in the chord structure (in this case the F position) is raised one half step for each fret gone up, thereby raising the complete chord by one half step. From the F position, can you find the following major chords of A, B, C, D, E, and F? Try it.

EXERCISE—*Making Bar Chords*

From the Fm position make the following chords: Gm, Bm, and Dm. See Figure 63A for answers.

From the D major position make the following chords: E, G, and C. See Figure 63B for answers.

From the G major (straight bar) position make the following chords: A, B, C, D, E, and F. See Figure 63C for answers.

From the G7 position make the following chords: A7, D7, and F#7. See Figure 63D for answers.

Answer to exercise:

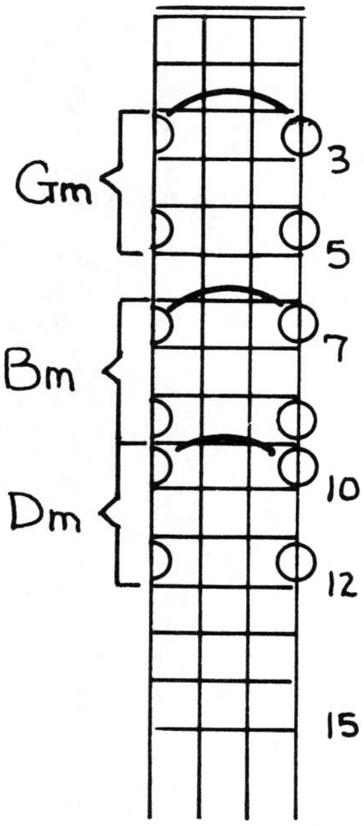

[Fig. 63A] 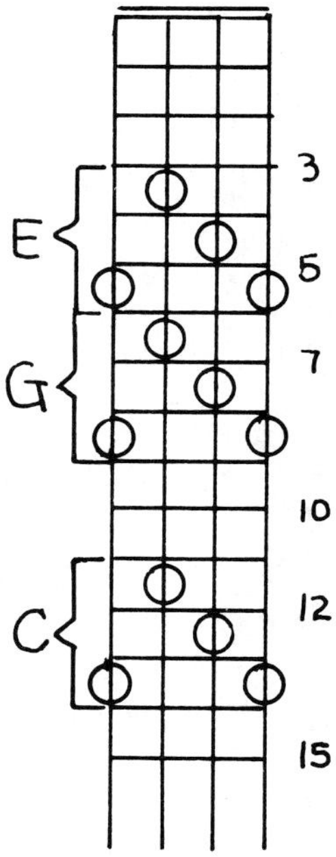   [Fig. 63B] 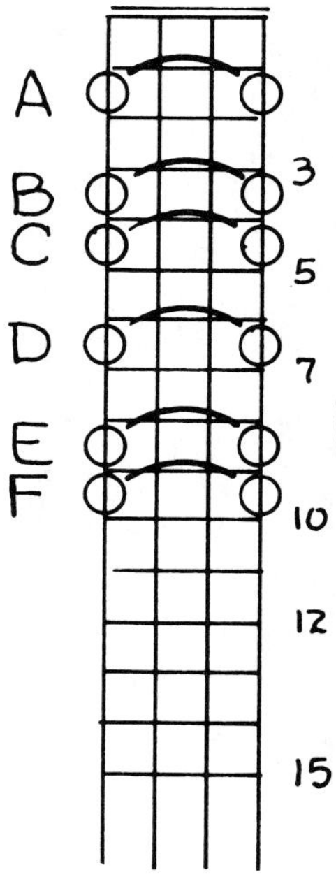   [Fig. 63C] 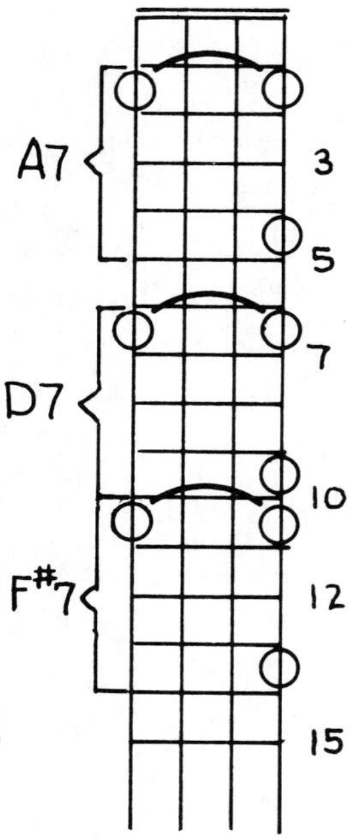   [Fig. 63D]

EXERCISE—*Songs in the Keys of C, D, A, E, and F*

Try your hand at these songs (each in a different key), using the floating-thumb double-thumbing technique.

Aunt Rhody

D   A7   D
Go tell Aunt Rhody, go tell Aunt Rhody

             G   A7   D
Go tell Aunt Rhody, the old grey goose is dead

The one she's been saving (3 times), to make her feather bed

The old gander's weeping (3 times), because his wife is dead

The goslings are mourning (3 times), because their mother's dead

She died in the millpond (3 times), from standing on her head

48

On Top of Old Smoky

```
C              F                    C
On top of old Smoky, all covered with snow
                    G7                 C
I lost my true lover, by courtin' too slow
```

Now courtin's a pleasure, and partin's a grief,
But a false-hearted lover's worse than a thief.

For a thief will just rob you, and take what you have,
But a false-hearted lover, will lead you to the grave.

And the grave will decay you, and turn you to dust,
Not one boy in a hundred, a poor girl can trust.

They'll hug you and kiss you, and tell you more lies,
Than cross-ties on a railroad, or stars in the skies.

So come all you young maidens, and listen to me,
Never place your affections, on a green willow tree

For the leaves they will wither, and the roots they will die,
And you'll all be forsaken, and never know why.

Rock-a My Soul

```
F
Rock-a my soul in the bosom of Abraham
C7
Rock-a my soul in the bosom of Abraham
F
Rock-a my soul in the bosom of Abraham
C7          F
Oh rock-a my soul
```

```
F                                    Second part (to be sung with above)
My heaven is so high, can't get over it
C7
So low, can't get under it
F
So wide, can't get around it
C7                          F
Gotta come in through the door
```

      A
Down the road here from me there's an old hollow tree

     D   **A**
Where you lay down a dollar or two.

If you hush up your mug they will fill up your jug

     E7   **A**
With that good old mountain dew.

           A
Chorus: They call it that good old mountain dew

           D   **A**
And them that refuse it are few.

You may go round the bend, but you'll come back again

          E7   **A**
For that good old mountain dew.

My brother Mort, he's sawed off and short
He measures just four foot two.
But he thinks he's a giant when they give him a pint
Of that good old mountain dew.

My Uncle Bill has a still on the hill,
Where he runs off a gallon or two.
The birds in the sky get so high they can't fly,
On that good old mountain dew.

The teacher came by with a tear in his eye,
Said his wife had the flu.
We told him he ought to give her a quart
Of that good old mountain dew.

My Aunt June has a brand new perfume,
It has such a sweet smelling pu.
Imagine her surprise when she had it analyzed,
It was that good old mountain dew.

Mister Roosevelt told me just how he felt,
The day the dry law went through.
"If your likker's too red, it will swell up your head,
Better stick to that mountain dew."

E   **Am**   E
Hava na gila, hava na gila, hava na gila, Vā nis-ma-ha (2 times)

E   **Dm**
Hava na re-ne-na, Hava na re-ne-na

                 E
      Hava na re-ne-na, Vā nis-ma-ha (2 times)

Am
Uru, uru, uru, Uru Ach-hem va lev sa-ma-ha

                   Dm
Ur ach-hem va lev sa-ma-ha, Uru ach-hem va lev sa-ma-ha

                   E
Uru ach-hem va lev sa-ma-ha, Uru ach-hem, Uru ach-hem

   E7   **Am**
Va lev sa-ma-a-a-ha

TRANSLATION:

hava = let us have	renena = shout out
na = to	uru = wake up
gila = joy	achem = brothers
vā or ve = short for hava	va = and
nismaha or samaha = happy	lev = hearts

Transposing

Again the relationship of music to mathematics can be demonstrated. One note is relative to another, and all the notes are in proportion or ratios to each other.

Let's say a song is written in the key of G and has the chords G, Em, C, and D7. However, the song is too low for your voice range. You would be comfortable singing the song in the key of C. But here is the dilemma: the song is written in the key of G, so you must change the key. The conversion process from the key of G to the key of C is known as "transposing."

Look at the CCC in Figure 4 and think of the twelve half steps as being chords rather than notes. The C chord is five half steps clockwise from the G chord according to the CCC. You can now transpose the other chords to the key of C:

- G + five half steps clockwise = C
- Em + five half steps clockwise = Am
- C + five half steps clockwise = F
- D7 + five half steps clockwise = G7

Now just play these new chords in place of the old ones and you will be playing the song in the key of C.

Note that:

- Major chord + x half steps = major chord
- Minor chord + x half steps = minor chord
- Seventh chord + x half steps = seventh chord

Keeping this in mind and assuming that you know enough chords, you can play any song in any key.

Let's take another example. Say you want to play in the key of D for a particular song, but the music for the song is written in the key of E. The chords are E, E7, Cm, A, and B7. We can see from the CCC that D is ten half steps clockwise from E; therefore, all the chords to be transposed will be ten half steps clockwise from the chords written to the music.

Now go to the chord transposition table (Fig. 64, Fig. 64 cont.) and find E in the "chord" column. Going horizontally, D is ten half steps above E; therefore, *all* the chords will be ten half steps above the chords written to the music.

CHORD TRANSPOSITION TABLE

Number of Half Steps

Chord	1	2	3	4	5	6	7	8	9	10	11	12
A	A#/Bb	B	C	C#/Db	D	D#/Eb	E	F	F#/Gb	G	G#/Ab	A
A#/Bb	B	C	C#/Db	D	D#/Eb	E	F	F#/Gb	G	G#/Ab	A	A#/Bb
B	C	C#/Db	D	D#/Eb	E	F	F#/Gb	G	G#/Ab	A	A#/Bb	B
C	C#/Db	D	D#/Eb	E	F	F#/Gb	G	G#/Ab	A	A#/Bb	B	C
C#/Db	D	D#/Eb	E	F	F#/Gb	G	G#/Ab	A	A#/Bb	B	C	C#/Db
D	D#/Eb	E	F	F#/Gb	G	G#/Ab	A	A#/Bb	B	C	C#/Db	D
D#/Eb	E	F	F#/Gb	G	G#/Ab	A	A#/Bb	B	C	C#/Db	D	D#/Eb
E	F	F#/Gb	G	G#/Ab	A	A#/Bb	B	C	C#/Db	D	D#/Eb	E
F	F#/Gb	G	C#/Ab	A	A#/Bb	B	C	C#/Db	D	D#/Eb	E	F
F#/Gb	G	G#/Ab	A	A#/Bb	B	C	C#/Db	D	D#/Eb	E	F	F#/Gb
G	G#/Ab	A	A#/Bb	B	C	C#/Db	D	D#/Eb	E	F	F#/Gb	G
G#/Ab	A	A#/Bb	B	C	C#/Db	D	D#/Eb	E	F	F#/Gb	G	G#/Ab

[Fig. 64]

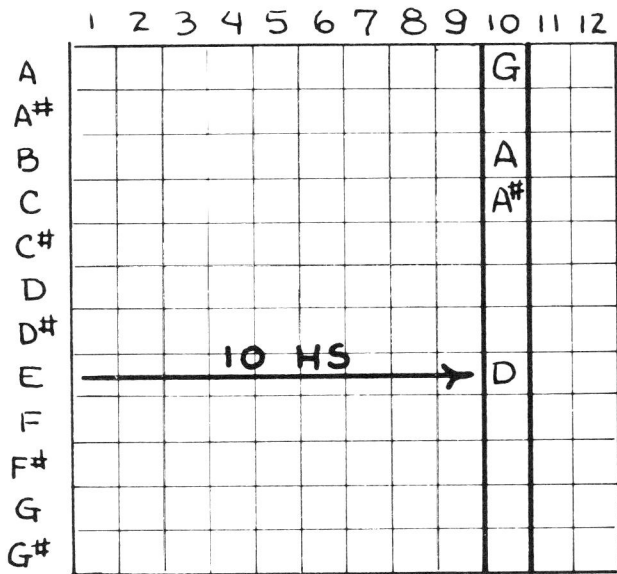

From the Chord Transposition Table:

From Key of E to Key of D = 10 HS

E + 10 HS = D

E7 + 10 HS = D7

Cm + 10 HS = A$^{\#}$m

A · + 10 HS = G

B7 + 10 HS = A7

[Fig. 64. Cont.]

[Fig. 65]

THE CAPO

The capo (Fig. 65) is an extremely useful accessory to the banjo, making it very easy to transpose from one key to another. It is a padded bar that is clamped onto the neck of the instrument. Capos range in price from $1 to $2.50. The basic function of this tool is to shorten the strings at various frets, thereby effectively making the banjo neck shorter.

For every fret the capo is moved up, the notes from the strings are raised one half step. Look at the open-G chord of Figure 66A. If the capo is placed on the first fret (actually between the nut and fret 1), each string is raised one half step, thereby making a G$^{\#}$ major chord. (See Fig. 66B.) If the capo is placed on the second fret and the strings played open, an A major chord sounds. (See Fig. 66C.)

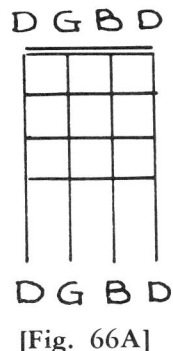

[Fig. 66A]

[Fig. 66B]

[Fig. 66C]

53

The capo can be thought of as a tool that can transfer you to various keys, while you continue to play the formations of another key. Here is an example: let's play a song in the key of C using the chord formations for the key of G. (What's that you say?)

Look at the chord transposition table (Fig. 64). In the chord column find G and travel horizontally until C is reached (five half steps). In other words, C is five half steps above G (Fig. 67).

[Fig. 67]

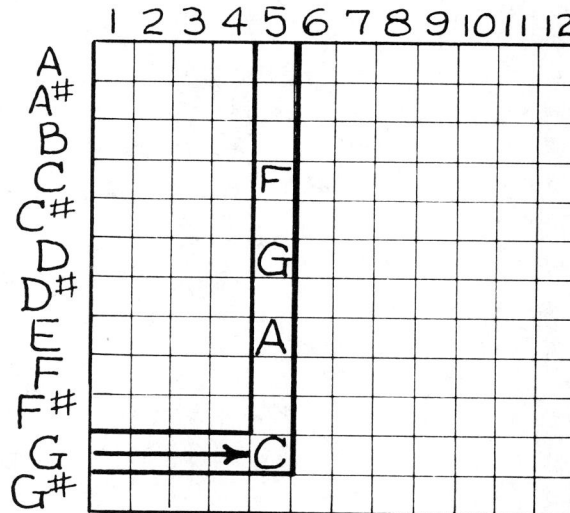

We already know that one half step equals one fret, so place the capo on the fifth fret and play the G chord (all strings open). What notes are being played? Notes C, E, and G, which make up a C major chord. (See Fig. 68A.)

When the C major chord for open-G tuning is played with the capo on the fifth fret, what chord is actually being played? The combination of F, A, and C notes make up the F major chord. (See Fig. 68B.) Note also from the chord transposition table (Fig. 64) that F is five half steps above C.

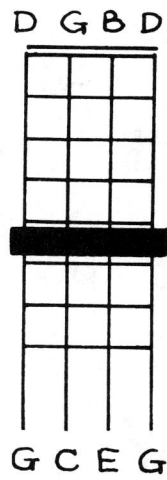

[Fig. 68A]

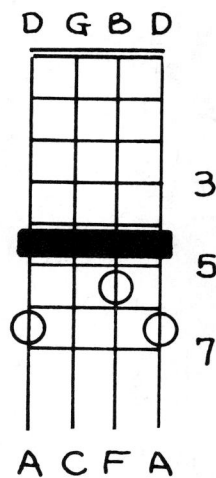

[Fig. 68B]

If an Em chord is played with the capo on the fifth fret, what chord is actually being played? An Am chord, right? If the D7 chord is played with the capo on the fifth fret, the G7 chord is played. (Check the chord transposition table again!)

But what does all this mean? Simple, if you know one key really well, say G, with the use of the capo you can play in any other of the eleven keys by moving the capo up the neck. Almost like cheating, isn't it? That is why the capo is also known as the "cheater."

If you use the capo much, you may want to invest in a fifth-string capo for your banjo. This special device capos the fifth string only. It enables that string to go up in pitch without tuning it up to the point of breaking. Fifth-string capos range anywhere from $7 to $35. Pete Seeger's book *How to Play the Five-String Banjo* shows how you can make a fifth-string capo with the use of screws.

Variations in Technique

DOUBLE-THUMBING WHILE STRUMMING

There is a technique I use all the time when I want to be heard in noisy bars and the like. It is a combination of double-thumbing and strumming and has the advantages of both; the double-thumbing part can pick the melody, while the strumming can keep a strong over-powering rhythm.

Rather than plucking a string with the thumb, strum down on the strings instead. Read "down" as going from string 5 to string 1. (See Fig. 69.) A quick strum is called a brush (Br).

[Fig. 69]

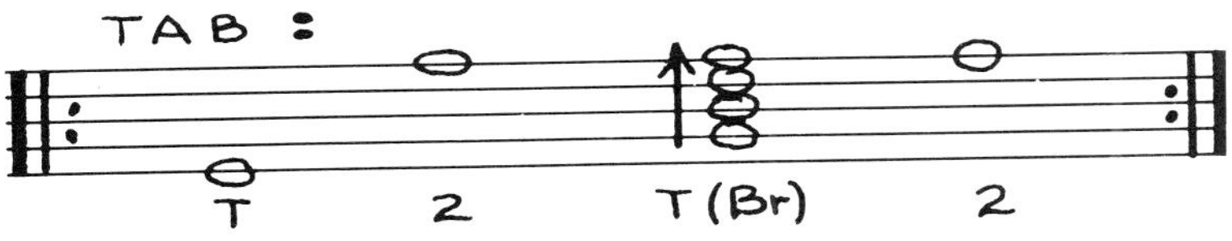

To pick the melody while double-thumbing and strumming, try the measure in Figure 70A. Still another variation is to strum down (string 5 to 1) with the thumb and up (string 1 to 5) with finger 2 (Fig. 70B).

[Fig. 70A]

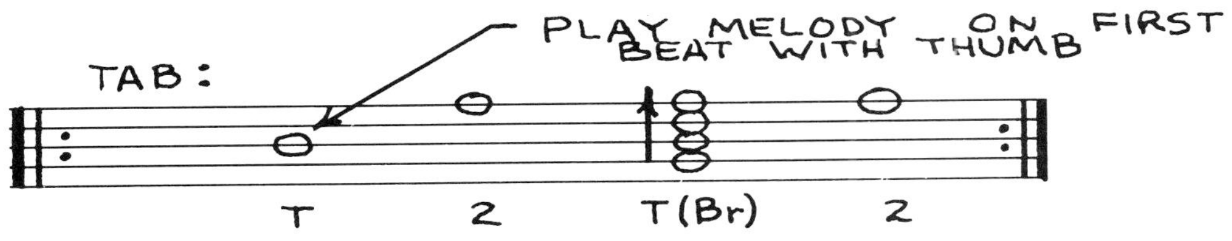

[Fig. 70B]

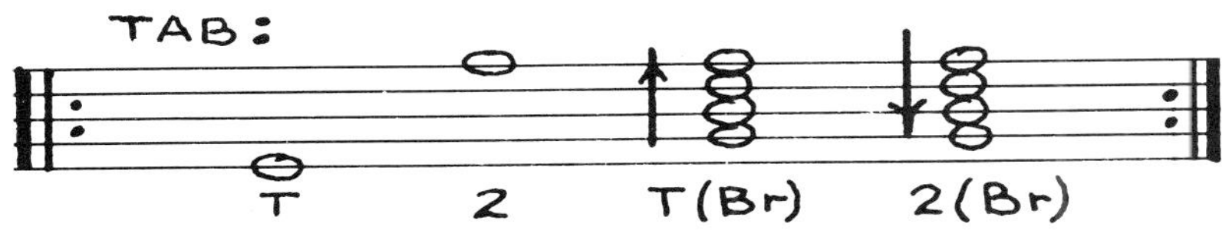

EXERCISE—*"Aunt Rhody"*

Most of our songs so far have been in the key of G. Let's try "Aunt Rhody" again (key of D) (Fig. 71). *Quick Quiz:* What is the major diatonic scale for the key of D? (See Fig. 41.)

Perform the following for "Aunt Rhody":

- Strum the *chords* through the song.
- Pick the *melody* with respect to the *chords* with the thumb.
- Double-thumb while strumming the song and fill in the tablature (Fig. 72). I have provided an arrangement (Fig. 73), but don't peek until you have written your own.

[Fig. 71]

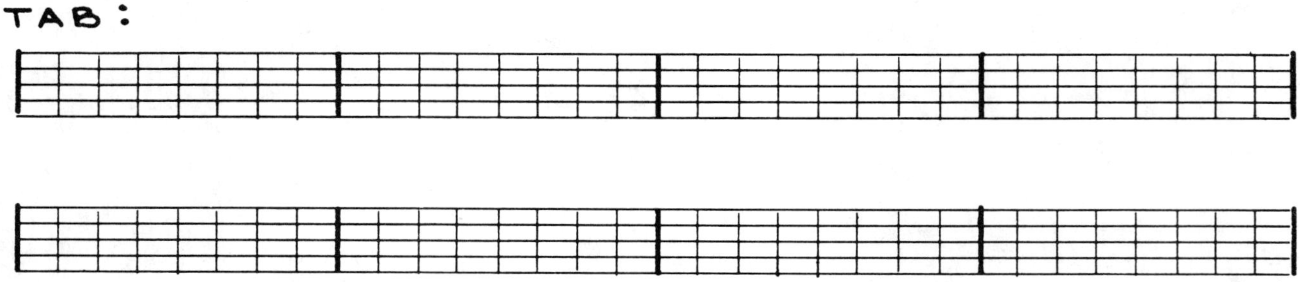

GO TELL AUNT RHO-DY, GO TELL AUNT RHO-DY,
GO TELL AUNT RHO-DY, THE OLD GREY GOOSE IS DEAD

TAB:

[Fig. 72]

Here is my solution to double-thumbing while strumming "Aunt Rhody." If it is not *exactly* the same as yours, don't worry about it; this is just one of many approaches to the song. What should be consistent is the melody with respect to the chords and the proper timing. An upward arrow indicates the down strum and a downward arrow indicates the up strum.

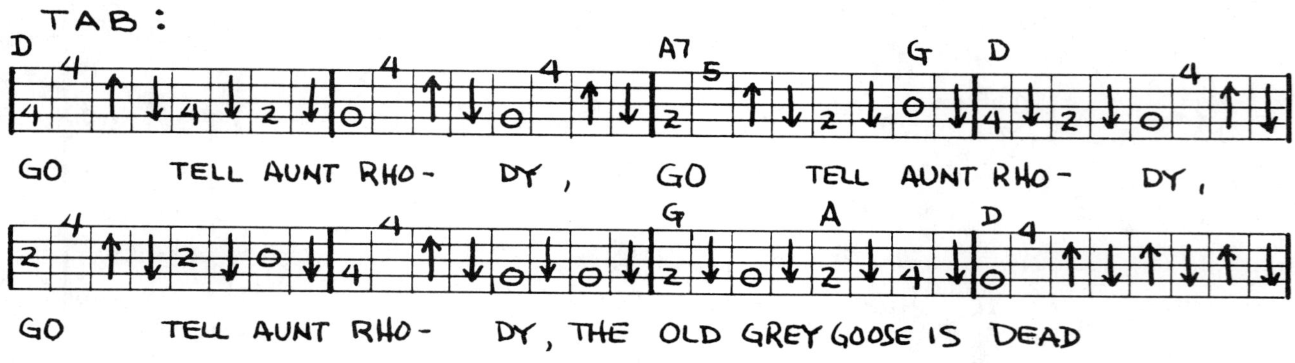

TAB:

GO TELL AUNT RHO- DY , GO TELL AUNT RHO- DY,
GO TELL AUNT RHO- DY, THE OLD GREY GOOSE IS DEAD

[Fig. 73]

HAMMERING-ON

A unique method of aiding and emphasizing the beat of a song is called "hammering-on." To hammer-on, simply pluck a string with the right hand then fret it with the left hand while the string is resonating. A higher note now sounds. Here you get two notes for the pluck of one!

A good example of hammering-on is to make a G chord (strings open). Pluck the fourth string with the right hand; while it is vibrating, hammer-on the left-hand social finger to the second fret of the fourth string. You have just hammered-on an E note to the open-D note string (Fig. 74).

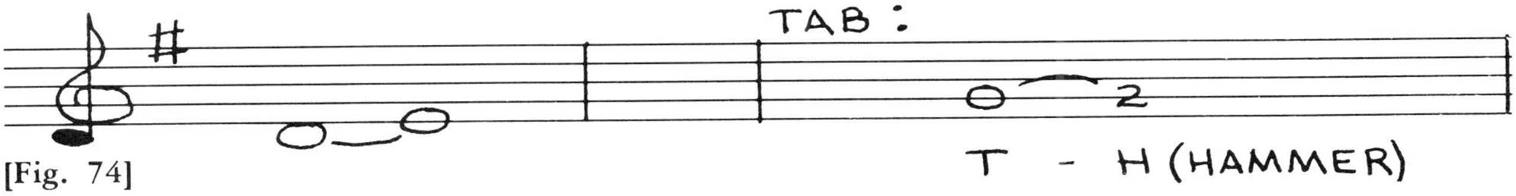

[Fig. 74]

Hammering-on can be used not only in plucking notes but also in strumming chords. When hammering-on while strumming, strum the unfretted strings and then hammer-on to a higher fret while the string is still resonating (Fig. 75).

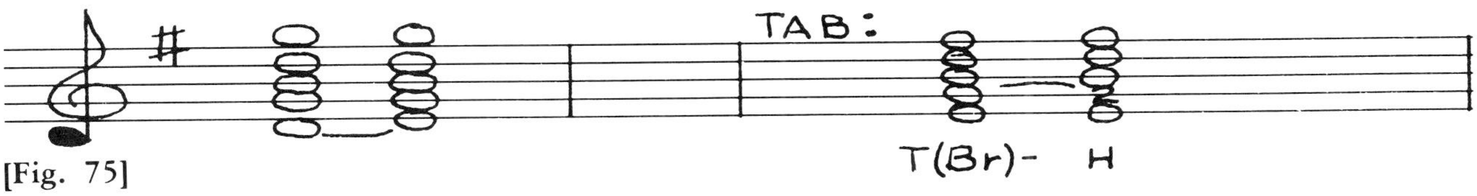

[Fig. 75]

PULLING-OFF

The antithesis of hammering-on is "pulling-off." Here again you can obtain many unique sounds and beat styles from pulling-off.

To pull-off, pull or pluck on a fretted string with one of your left-hand fingers and make that string vibrate unfretted.

Try this. Form a D7 chord. Now pluck the second string (C note). While it is still vibrating, with finger 1 of the left hand pluck the second string to sound the open B note. Again, two notes for the pluck of one (Fig. 76).

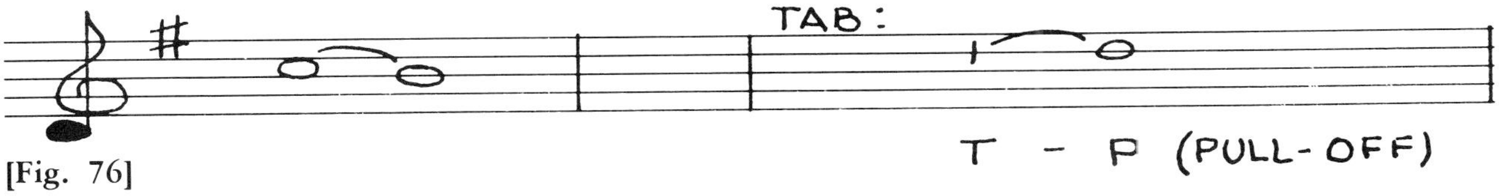

[Fig. 76]

Pulling-off can also be used in strumming or brushing. After you get a good feel for pulling-off, you can develop your own technique. Here again, pulling-off, like hammering-on, can give added emphasis to a song arrangement and make it sound very complex even though it is very easy to accomplish.

It is time to kick you out of the nest! By now, I hope you have the hang of how to approach a song. Now is the time for you to try another music book and apply the three-step approach:

- Strum the chords of the song.
- Pick the melody with respect to the chords.
- Apply a right-hand style such as double-thumbing or Seeger style (coming up next).

SEEGER STYLE

The old barn-dance type of playing is what I call Seeger style, since Pete has used it throughout the years and the style is identified with his playing. This method brings out the unique characteristic of the five-string banjo by the continuous sounding of the fifth string "drone tone."

There are four steps to Seeger style:

- With finger 1, pluck up on the fourth string open.
- Hammer-on the second fret of the fourth string.
- Brush down on the strings (usually the third, second, and first) with the right-hand fingernail of finger 2 or 3.
- Pluck down on the fifth string with the thumb.

There are four whole beats to this style. Each of the four steps above gets a whole beat (Fig. 77).

[Fig. 77]

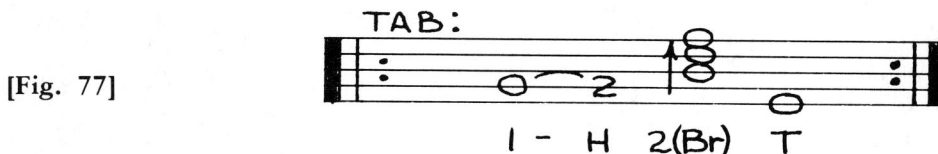

The sound made is "ba-room-di-dy." Finger 1 is good for two whole beats. Start very slowly making four equal distinct beats. Don't worry about speed, it comes with *much, much practice.*

Count out loud, 1, 2, 3, 4. For each count play one beat at a time until it sounds smooth; 1, 2, 3, 4 = ba-room-di-dy.

Now apply this style to the songs in the book or your own favorites. The melody will be played by finger 1, rather than the thumb as in double-thumbing.

When you reach a certain speed, you will no longer want to hammer-on (you will be going so fast you won't be able to!). However, finger 1 still plays two whole beats. It now sounds like "boom-di-dy."

EXERCISE—*Chords Played Seeger Style*

Following are some exercises using the Seeger style. These include the keys with their associated chords along with hammering-on and pulling-off (Fig. 78).

TAB: KEY OF G
G
C
1-H BrT 1- BrT 1-H BrT 1- BrT 1-H BrT 1- Br T 1-H BrT 1- BrT
D7
G
1-H BrT 1- BrT 1-H BrT 1- BrT 1-H BrT 1- BrT 1-H BrT 1- BrT
TAB: KEY OF C
C
F
G7
C
1- BrT 1- BrT 1- BrT 1- BrT 1- BrT 1-P BrT 1- BrT 1—
TAB: KEY OF D
D
G
A7
D
1-P BrT 1- BrT 1-P BrT 1- BrT 1- BrT 1- BrT 1- BrT 1—
TAB: KEY OF A
A
D
E7
A
1- BrT 1- BrT 1- BrT 1- BrT 1- BrT 1- BrT 1- BrBr
TAB: KEY OF E
E
A
B7
E
1-H BrT 1- BrT 1-H BrT 1- BrT 1- BrT 1- BrT 1-H BrT 1—

[Fig. 78]

EXERCISE—"Darlin' Cory" Played Seeger Style

"Darlin' Cory" is an old mountain standard that is traditionally played in the Seeger style (Fig. 79).

First, pick the melody with finger 1. The song is in 2/2 time, so a half note gets a whole beat.

Play the melody on the first string for the D note (second line from the top on the treble clef scale) and notes above D. The lines above the treble clef scale are called "ledger" lines. They are simply an extension of the treble clef scale (Fig. 80).

WAKE UP WAKE UP DAR-LIN' CO- RY

WHAT MAKES YOU SLEEP SO SOUND

THE REV- E- NUE OF-FI- CERS COM- MIN'

GON- NA TEAR YOUR STILL HOUSE DOWN

[Fig. 79]

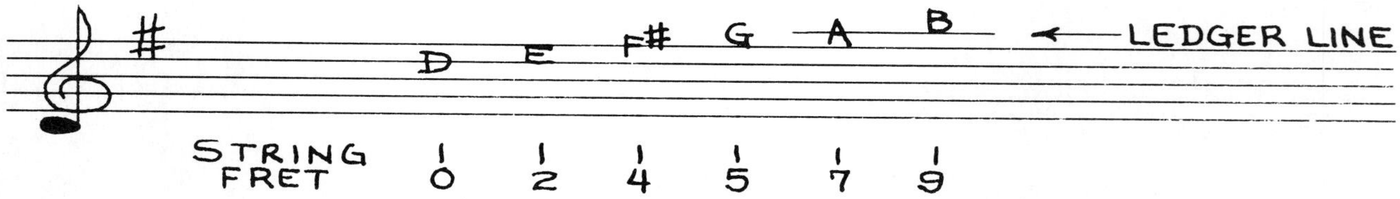

D E F# G A B ← LEDGER LINE

STRING 1 1 1 1 1 1
FRET 0 2 4 5 7 9

[Fig. 80]

Let each half note equal the four full beats of the Seeger-style riff of "1-and-Br-T." That is, a half note equals "1-and-Br-T." Therefore, a quarter note equals "1-and" and the next quarter note equals "Br-T." The two half notes "tied" together are equivalent to a whole note, or two full Seeger-style riffs of "1-and-Br-T-1-and-Br-T."

The thirteenth measure is played by moving the F chord up two frets to make the G chord. In this position, the D note for "gon-na" and "still" is located on the third fret of the second string, the G note for "tear your" is located on the first string of the fifth fret, and the B note for "house" is located on the third string of the fourth fret (Fig. 62C). The sixteenth measure goes back to the open-string G chord.

Play this song first from your rendition, then compare it to the arrangement that follows (Fig. 81). A break between verses of the song is given below the arrangement. It is one of many for the key of G. Try some of your own.

TAB:

G

WAKE UP WAKE UP DAR-LIN' CO- -RY

WHAT MAKES YOU SLEEP SO SOUND

F

THE REV-E- NUE OF-FI- CERS COM- MIN'

G/F3

G

GON- NA TEAR YOUR STILL HOUSE DOWN

I Br T I Br T I Br T I Br T I Br T I Br T I Br T I Br T

I-P Br T I-P Br T I-P Br T I-P Br T I-P Br T I-P Br T I-P Br T I— Br T

[Fig. 81]

61

If A Is May, F# Must Be February

Remember when the chromatic circle cycle (CCC) was introduced, it was likened to a clock showing twelve hours (half steps). Now let's look at another relationship.

The number "12" reoccurs in many of life's realms. Could it be a cosmic number? It is found in:

- Time—12 hours in a day and in a night. One earth revolution = 2 × 12 hours. One earth revolution around the sun = 12 months = one year.
- Religion—12 tribes of Israel; 12 Apostles of Christ.
- Mythology—astrology's 12 zodiac signs.
- Music—12 half steps in music = one revolution = one octave.

Is there some relation between sound (musical notes) and time (months of the year)? I think so.

Let's take one final look at the CCC. Assign the month of May to note A and proceed clockwise for succeeding months (Fig. 82). The key of C is the only key without any sharps or flats, so its major diatonic scale is C, D, E, F, G, A, and B. The corresponding months of August, October, December, January, March, May, and July are the only months with 31 days!

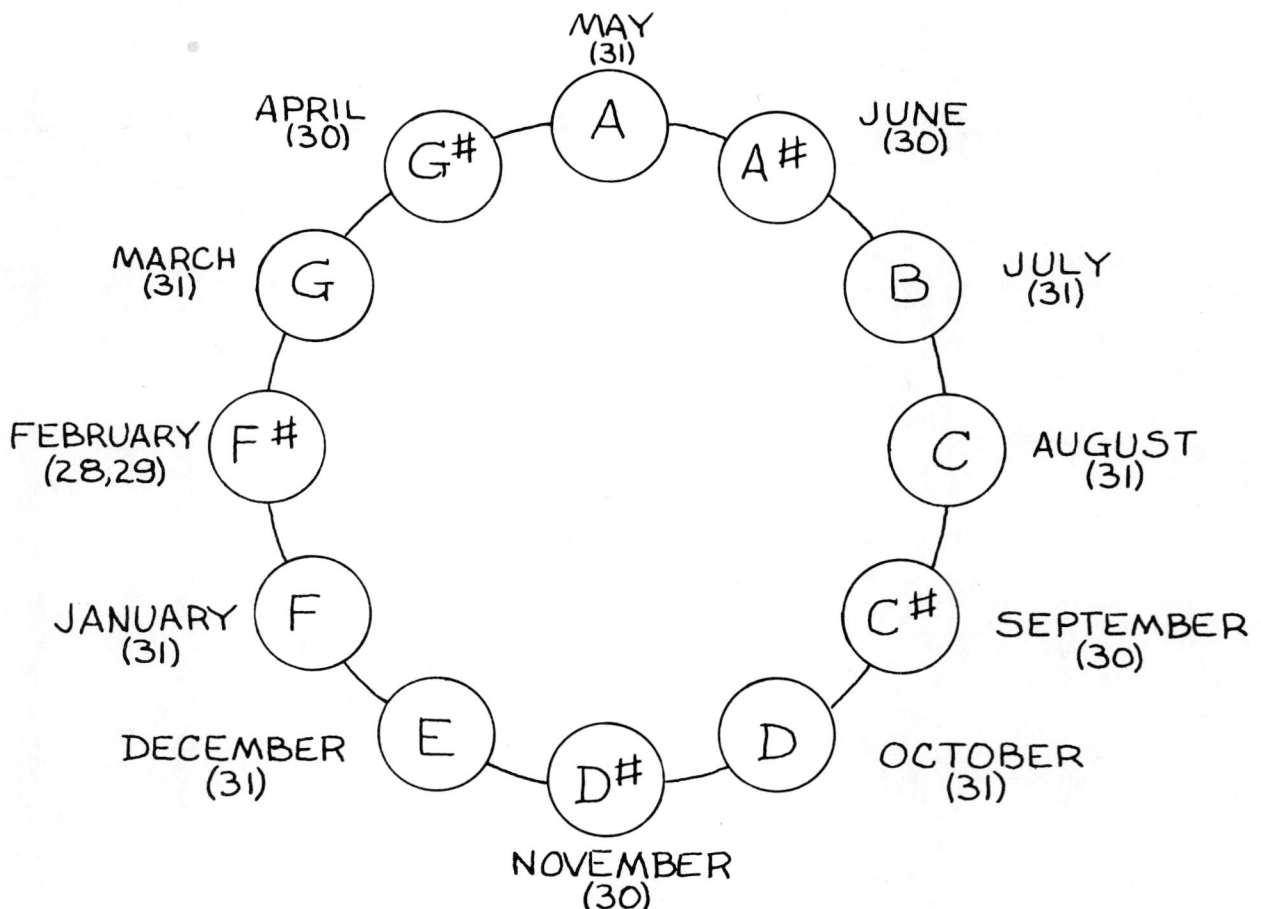

[Fig. 82]

Still not convinced? February is the only month that changes every leap year from 28 to 29 days. It is the compromising month. In music, when tuning up a piano, all the other notes are exact except for one that must be a compromise to keep the others in the proper proportions. It is F#.